The Lost Art of

Human
Memory

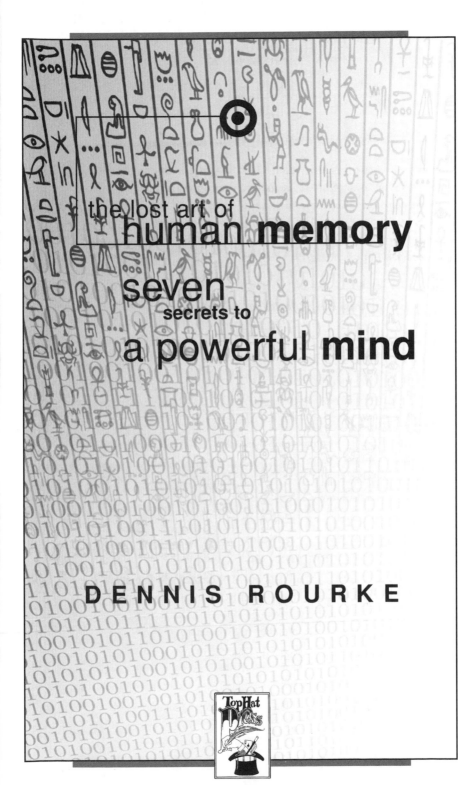

the lost art of
human **memory**

seven
secrets to
a powerful **mind**

DENNIS ROURKE

TopHat
Press

The Lost Art of Human Memory
A Powerful Mind

ISBN 0-9679282-0-6

Publisher's Cataloging-in-Publication
(Provided by Quality Books, Inc.)
Rourke, Dennis, 1946-
    The lost art of human memory / Dennis Rourke.
  -- 1st ed.
    p.cm.
    Includes index.
    ISBN: 0-9679282-0-6

    1. Mnemonics. 2. Memory. I. Title.

BF385.R68 2000   153.1'4
                  QBI00-414

ATTENTION COMPANIES, ORGANIZATIONS, ASSOCIATIONS AND SCHOOLS:

Discounts are available on bulk purchases of this book for premiums, sales promotions, educational purposes or fund raising. Custom printing or excerpts can also be provided to meet specific needs.
For more information, please contact:

Top Hat Press
P.O. Box 641888
Omaha, NE 68164

Toll-free 1-877-841-2935 • website: powerfulmind.com

DEDICATION

To my dear wife Ann
and my children, Sean and Shannon
who have given me so
much worth remembering.

ACKNOWLEDGEMENTS

Illustrations
Wayne Sealy

Editing
Rebecca Rotert

Cover Design
Turnpost Design

Typesetting
Linda Fausset

Photos
Vern Goff

Author's photo
James Scholz

Models for 'Names' photos:
Mark Darby, RN
Scharlie Fitts
Sylvia Kessler
Mary Kay Mueller
Mark Peterson, PhD
Joe Pittman
Ann Scholz
Crystall Williams
Vern Wirka

A MOST ANCIENT AND MAGICAL ART

In the dim reaches of antiquity, people taught their young, conducted business and recorded their history without the benefit of a written language. Indeed, for most of human history, there was no alphabet. Even the bible was passed intact from generation to generation for a thousand years before the Hebrew people had a written language.

Before the days of writing, educated people learned just as much as they do today, if not more. However, they kept what they learned in their minds rather than on paper or computer. Their command of knowledge would make them seem like prodigies by today's standards. However, it was not genius, but training that gave them such powerful minds.

A wonderful science of memory was well developed and commonly known in ancient times. It is all but lost today. That body of techniques is called "Mnemonics" (pronounced Neh MON iks.) Mnemonic systems were taught at an early age and built upon as a child grew. Families, clans, schools and churches had memory systems common to their members.

Learned people cultivated and developed a strong memory because it was the seat of all knowledge. Art, literature, laws, and the crafts of each occupation were all contained in the memory of the people.

One of the oldest systems of mnemonics still in use today is the imagery of the constellations. The signs of the Zodiac were actually devices to help people remember the path of the sun and planets. They were also used in ancient times as a set of hooks to remember other types of information.

The first written languages were, in fact, more akin to mnemonics than to a phonetic alphabet. These languages used commonly accepted symbols to express ideas rather than sound. Some early scripts were no doubt just a visual representation of the mnemonics already in everyday use. Even with the coming of the written word, mnemonics remained common among the educated class. Paper was, until quite recently, a scarce commodity and far too expensive to be used for recording what one should remember anyway.

There were great treatises on mnemonics in classical times. Cicero in "The Art of Memory" described the great memory feats of Simonides of Ceos who lived in the 5th century BC. Simonides was said to have been able to remember thousands of poems. Cicero himself was highly regarded for his ability to remember the names of everyone he met. Other authors on memory included Quintilian, Socrates, Plato and Seneca.

Much later, in the 13th century, Thomas Aquinas elevated the skill to the level of a virtue in his "Summa Theologiae." He considered Cicero's Art of Memory as an element of prudence.

In medieval times the Dominican order was known for its memory training. The secret of that training was revealed by Giordano Bruno, who upon leaving the order, published "On the Shadows of Ideas" in 1582.

Today, amidst the world of computer servers and Internet communication, the "Art of Memory" is all but forgotten. The human mind, however, still retains all of the traits that made that skill possible. Practitioners of mnemonics have refined and polished the skill over eons of use. Those skills and their modern applications are the subject of this book.

Armed with those skills you will be able to remember what you see, hear and read with incredible accuracy. You will be able to learn with astounding speed.

You are now about to learn a most ancient and powerful discipline. Enjoy your discovery of this lost art and all of the advantages it brings you.

***

TABLE OF CONTENTS

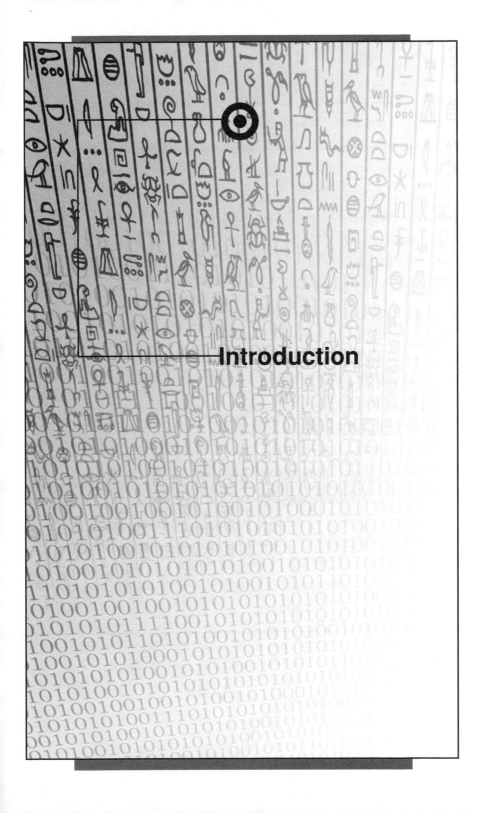

Introduction

Let me tell you about my personal journey towards a greater memory. In high school, I was what you might call an average student. My grades were good, but certainly not good enough to gain scholarships.

It had always been assumed in our family that the children would go to college. There was a war on when my parents came of age so neither of them had attended college. However, they wanted that for their children.

With seven kids in the family, there was no money for college. My dad, unable to afford college for his kids, did the most amazing thing. To this day I marvel at his wisdom, though I did not understand it at the time.

What he did was enroll in college himself. Without ever saying so, he made certain that we would attend college. Because he was working and raising a family while attending school, we couldn't drop out. We had no excuse. It was no harder for us to attend than it was for him.

So I enrolled in school, took classes in the morning, and operated a punch press at night. It was hard. What free time I had, I used for studying. I got good grades, but it was tough. I was always tired.

At the end of that year another funny thing happened. Like many a young man I felt I had a calling to the priesthood. In the fall I went away to the seminary. Time to study was no longer in short supply, but there was a lot more to study.

It was in Fr. Martin's religion class that the first revelation came. Father Martin had just called on a friend of mine. Jim stood up and instead of answering the question said, "Father, I'm not sure I understood that portion of the study." Father Martin looked at Jim, pulled his glasses down on his nose, and asked, "What portion of the material did you not understand?"

Jim shifted his shoulders back and forth, shuffled his feet a bit and began to sweat. Father Martin just waited until Jim finally said, "Uh,... the whole concept, Father."

Father Martin's asked, "Do you mean Transubstantiation? "Yeah, Father," said Jim. Father Martin then asked," Did you read the assignment, Mr. Roberts?"

"Yes, Father."

"Well, Mr. Roberts, did you not read page 124?"

"Yes, Father."

"And you read the third paragraph down from the top?"

"Uh, maybe I missed that, Father." Jim's face was bright red now. Father Martin let him sit down.

Two things became quite clear to me. First, there is a way to memorize whole books, though you might have to be a monk to do it. I didn't have a clue how he did it. Secondly, I learned you don't want to go to Father Martin's class unprepared.

The next revelation was the clincher. In a book swap, I picked up a book on memory. When I finally got around to reading it I discovered something truly remarkable. With a little bit of practice I could use the techniques in the book to memorize lots of stuff very quickly.

The guy who loaned me the book had not read it. He was just as amazed as I was. Together we worked out a system of hooks and studied for Professor Green's history final using the system. We got the top scores in class. No one else came close. It did occur to Professor Green that we might have cheated. But, he quizzed us verbally and then congratulated us. We were in heaven. We had not spent a great deal of time studying but had both gotten an A+.

I now understood a very precious secret. The mind could be developed just as easily as the muscles could, perhaps even more easily. We all have tremendous memory capacity that we never use.

Later, I left the seminary and returned to regular college. I still went to class in the morning and worked at the factory by night. But now, as I repeated the monotonous steps to operate my machine, I was reviewing my notes from class. The notes were not on paper, but in my head. Now the small amount of study time was adequate. In fact, I started taking more classes.

Here are some other examples of powerful minds.

SHANNON'S ART HISTORY CLASS

The students of Ms. Ellison's Art History class nervously shuffled to their desks. In just a few minutes they would take the final exam worth 25% of their grade for the semester.

There were complaints that the test was just too hard. There were over 100 slides of works they had studied. Many different periods, artists and styles were represented. The students would be shown 35 slides. They would then be asked to identify the name of the work, the subject, the artist, the country and the period. This was not a multiple-choice test. They had to know the material.

For most, this was a required course and they had been studying for weeks. Several students had been up half of the night studying. One student, Shannon, spent only half an hour reviewing her notes and then went out for pizza. She got a 98% on the test. The next highest score was 74%. The curve was ruined, but Shannon was guaranteed an 'A' for the semester.

Shannon was suspected of cheating on the test. Ms. Ellison called her into her office and asked her how she got such a high score. She even quizzed her on the material over again to make sure she knew it. Her command of the material was almost flawless.

Was Shannon a genius or a child prodigy in the area of Art History? No. She does equally well in most of her classes. What is her secret?

She used a systematic approach to learning the material. Before starting college Shannon had learned and practiced a memory system called 'Mnemonics.' That practice long ago made memorization very easy for her. She could commit a lot of information to memory very quickly and retain it for as long as she needed. She no longer relies on rote memory. Her memory is highly organized and very quick. Because of that she has a very thorough understanding of the things she studies.

THERE'S SOMETHING ABOUT ROGER

Roger is the kind of guy that everyone likes. That's why Roger is such a successful salesman. Roger always seems like someone that you've known all of your life. Even when you first meet him, he seems to know you. He calls you by name. You may not remember his name, but that's because there were seven or eight people introduced at once. Roger, however, calls everyone by name. It makes you like him.

Roger has a lot of skills that make him a great salesman, but one of them is his amazing memory for names. Roger got that way by taking a course in memory skills that emphasized the recollection of names. Over the years he has become quite good at it.

FATHER JIM'S AMAZING MEMORY

Father Jim is a parish priest who has developed a reputation as an excellent speaker. His church is filled to overflowing every Sunday morning. Father is also on demand as a retreat master at monasteries, convents and religious gatherings around the country. The retreats call for him to speak for several hours per day for three days on end. His subject matter varies from group to group.

There are many elements to Father Jim's ability to hold an audience. He is a very able speaker. But one thing that always strikes people is that he never speaks from notes. He does not stand behind a podium, or lectern. He stands at the front of his audience with empty hands and speaks to them almost intimately. One wonders how he can speak so eloquently and at such length without a prepared text.

In truth, Father has prepared his material. He has written, refined, and organized it just as any speaker would. However, he commits the entirety of it to memory before he meets his audience. It does not take a long time; in fact he has admitted that he frequently changes what he will say based on what happens during a retreat. He then re-memorizes what he is going to talk about during a break. How can he do this?

Father Jim, long ago, learned how to use a memory system we call 'Landmarks'. It is a fairly simple memory system, which he has perfected into a highly refined mental skill. It is one of the tools that makes him such a great speaker.

YOUR MEMORY

This book will teach you how to develop the type of memory skill that Shannon, Roger and Father Jim use so well. It does not require a gift or a very high IQ. Regular practice and application of the skills are all that's needed. You won't need to practice for hours per day. Fifteen to thirty minutes per day will yield excellent results.

MAPPING THE MIND

The human memory is a huge repository of knowledge. Its proportions are so vast that we frequently get lost within it. We forget where things are or lose our way to the information we know is there.

It helps to think of our memory as our hometown. We all learn to get around in our neighborhood or city by mapping it out in our mind. We are not necessarily conscious of this mapping.

We learn where the major thoroughfares are, which streets run north and south or east and west. We position landmarks in our mind. We know where things are from a certain intersection, or the mall. We know if something is near Mary's house. We also learn how the buildings are numbered on a given street and how those numbers change on either side of a centerline.

Having imposed a system to our surroundings, it is much easier to navigate our neighborhood. Given an address, we can find it by applying our system.

It is possible to apply the same sort of system to our mind. We can establish landmarks, map the avenues, and even number the addresses of our memory. Then we can park what we learn at a particular intersection. When we need to find it again, we just follow our map to the right place and retrieve it.

HOW TO USE THIS BOOK

This is not the type of book to read in one or two sittings. Short measured bursts will serve you much better. The first and most important of the seven secrets to a better memory, is the basic principle of Tricking The Mind. You will learn about this in the first chapter.

The next six secrets concern basic skills that should be practiced regularly until you are comfortable with them. They are Linking, Reading, Landmarks, Hooks, Numbering, and Names. Time spent learning these core skills will significantly improve your memory.

There is no limit to the ways of applying the seven secrets. Remembering names, for instance, is an application of both the Landmarks and Linking. The most powerful memory systems are combinations of two or more of the basic. Learn the seven secrets well and you will be able to do truly amazing things with the combinations.

Some skills will be more difficult than others. Each one is important. Take time to practice each skill until it becomes comfortable. You don't have to be expert at a skill before you move to the next one, but you should be familiar with it.

For best results, apply the techniques to what you are learning now. Use the linking method to memorize new material you are studying or learning. Memorize a set of hooks and use it to learn something new. There are exercises at the end of each chapter that you can use to apply the individual skills. They are designed to help you apply the skills you just learned.

You need not use these exercises if you have something else you are interested in learning. Simply memorize that material using these techniques. You will find that regular practice makes you very proficient.

***

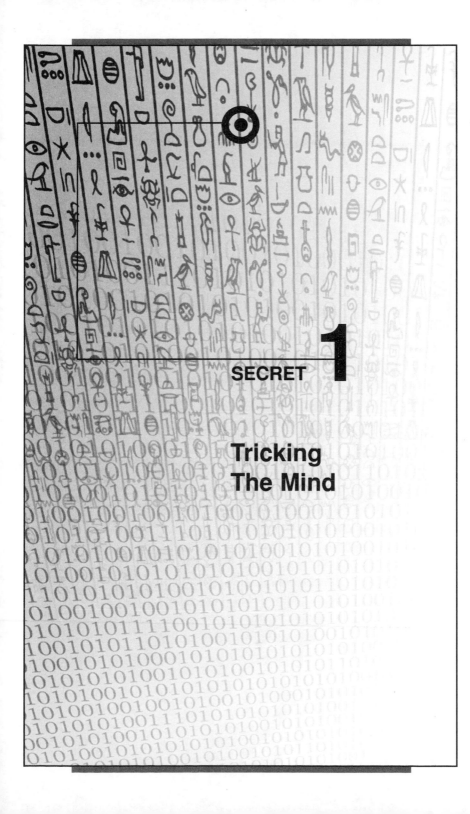

SECRET

1

Tricking
The Mind

SECRET 1
Tricking the Mind

It's fascinating how much information the average brain carries. If you think of your own career, it takes 12 to 20 years of schooling just to get ready. Then you absorb several years of experience under a variety of conditions. That's not to mention all the people you know and all that you know about them. If you had to print all that you know, you would denude a couple acres of trees just to make the paper. We have an awesome memory capacity.

It's estimated that we have the equivalent of 2000 volumes of memory space in our heads. Einstein, it is said, used less than ten percent of his brain. Most of us use far less than that. Obviously, running out of memory space, is something we don't need to worry about.

The brain seems to be rather selective, though, in how fast it learns something. Some things we learn like videotape. Once we see it, we have it forever. Others are like trying to chisel it in stone. It takes a long time and lots of strokes to get it down.

Many of us forget our own license number or zip code. Yet, we can remember the numbers of our birth date. We can also recall where we were and what we were doing when we heard about the Challenger disaster or some other tragedy, but not where we were last Tuesday.

The secret to remembering what we want is to trick the brain into thinking it is remembering one of those things that are easy to remember.

MNEMONICS

Marking the way:

Think of a trip by airplane. Suppose that you have just bought a ticket and the agent has taken your luggage. The ticket clerk points over your shoulder and says, "The plane will be at one of the gates over there."

You look, but there are no numbers and no signs. You just have to walk until you see your plane. It's there, but you have a terrible time finding it.

Of course, in real life, the gates are all numbered. There is a letter code or color code to tell you what concourse to take. Signs point the way and identify all the stops. Everything is laid out according to a system.

Finding things in our memory also works much better if we lay things out according to a system. We set up sign posts or letter codes to show the way and number the things we want to find later. To some degree, we all do some form of this already.

Tricks we already use

The practice of consciously associating items in the memory is called MNEMONICS and it is as old as humanity itself. We have all used it many times.

If someone were to ask right now how many days there are in August, chances are you are already reciting a poem. "Thirty days has September, April, June and November. All the rest have thirty one, save February with twenty eight." Or you might be counting the months on your knuckles.

Similarly, you probably recite a short rhyme when you start to spell 'receive.'

If asked the lines of the musical scale you might say, "Every good boy deserves fudge." The first letter of each word gives you the letter for the line in the scale.

That poem or knuckle trick for the calendar or phrase for the spelling of believe is a mnemonic, a device to bring something to mind that is not easy to remember. Think of how long ago you learned that trick. It has held that information accurately in your mind for a span of many years.

Here is a list of some of the more common and not so common memory tricks:

Item	Memory Trick
To spell "Receive" or "Believe."	"I before E, except after C.
The names of the great lakes.	**HOMES** (Huron, Ontario, Michigan, Erie, Superior)
Order of general ranks in the military.	**Be My Little General** (Brigadier, Major, Lieutenant, General)
The order of planets	**M**other **V**ery **E**agerly **M**ade **A** **J**elly **S**andwich **U**nder **N**o **P**rotest. (Mercury, Venus, Earth, Mars, Asteroids, Jupiter, Saturn, Uranus, Neptune, Pluto)

The Lost Art of Human Memory

Item	Memory Trick
The order of operations in algebra.	Please Excuse My Dear Aunt Sally. (Parentheses, Exponents, Multiplication, Division, Addition, Subtraction.)
Predicting weather by color.	Red sky in the morning, sailors take sky warning. Red sky at night, sailor's delight.
Order of suits in Bridge	New Sweethearts Happily Dance Close. (No Trump, Spades, Hearts, Diamonds, Clubs.)

You might say these sentences are merely tricking the memory. That's correct. We are merely tricking the memory. But it works, and it works very well. The art of tricking the memory is called Mnemonics. It is an art that is thousands of years old and its principles are simple and fun to apply.

The one unifying element of all of these memory tricks is that they are applied when you learn the thing. Otherwise, it is of no use when you want to recall the item. In other words, remembering is something you do up front to help you recall.

In the examples above we see very specific mnemonics. "Please Excuse My Dear Aunt Sally," is only used to memorize the order of operations in algebra. You can't use it to memorize the order of the planets, or the species of hominids. There is, however, a system that is designed to be adaptable to the material you need to learn. Once a person becomes practiced at this skill, anything can be committed to memory in exquisite detail.

6

Obviously the mind is good at remembering some things. Other things, it finds much tougher to remember. We can take advantage of what the mind remembers well and use it to remember what is difficult.

What are we good at remembering? That varies considerably from person to person. Generally, though, the following things are easy to remember:

Places.

We can all visualize places in our home, offices, schools, streets, churches, etc. We can remember a complicated route from one place to another.

Excitement.

Sudden loud noises, objects moving toward us rapidly, danger, passion, victory and surprise are all things we find hard to ignore and thus easy to remember.

Embarrassing moments.

The party we are most likely to remember is the one where we spilled a drink in our lap or dropped our glasses in the punchbowl.

Painful experiences.

No one forgets what it's like to have a tooth pulled or a bone set.

Things that don't fit or work properly.

Have you ever try to build something that was missing key components?

Silly or humorous events.

Have you ever thought of something funny during a funeral?

Our minds like to remember these things. What makes us laugh, what we fear, things that embarrass us jump to mind readily. Common ordinary items, though, hide in the clutter of everyday experience. In other words, we remember that which triggers our emotions.

Emotions are like markers in the mind. They are easily remembered so they can teach us survival skills in a hurry. Even a baby needs only one experience to learn not to touch the hot stove.

Consider one of our primitive ancestors walking through the woods. A strange new sound strikes her ears. It is a loud, blood-curdling roar. A large cat bounds toward her from the underbrush. Fear takes hold and her blood is filled with adrenaline. Quickly she scrambles up a tree narrowly escaping death.

Assuming she survives, she will always remember what that roar means. She will think of that beast whenever she comes to that place; remembering where she was, where she was going, who was with her, what the beast looked like, what smells were in the air, and whether it was cloudy or sunny.

She doesn't intend to remember all those things, but it happens. Her mind associates all of them together. One item will automatically remind her of the others, particularly the beast that made the roar.

We needn't put our lives in danger to remember effectively, but as you will see strong emotions and association can help a great deal. In fact, we can use this principle to great advantage.

***

SECRET 2

Linking

SECRET 2
Linking

W e'll now learn a set of systems that use emotions and silly pictures to deal with lots of different memory tasks. The first of these is the linking system. The easiest way to learn the linking system is to just do it.

Let's memorize a list, then we'll see how this works. Look at the following list but don't try to memorize it just yet. Let me talk you through it.

Bubble	Baseball
Rabbit	Hawk
Car	Glasses
Fish	Purse
Coffee cup	Dancer

Look at the following pictures and imagine the scenes.

Now I'll ask you to use your imagination. You are reading a book now. Use this book to remind you of the first item on the list.

Picture the book in a big bubble.

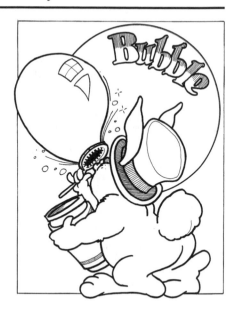

Now picture the rabbit blowing a big bubble, much bigger than she is. You should have just these two items in your picture.

Next, picture the rabbit driving a car. Again, just those two items.

Then imagine your car is made of a fish.

Then, picture a coffee cup with a big fish swimming in it.

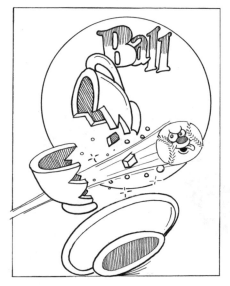

Visualize now a baseball smacking a full cup of coffee.

Now, see a hawk catching the baseball.

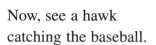

Now picture the hawk wearing glasses.

Imagine a purse wearing glasses.

Finally, picture a ballerina dancing with the purse over her shoulder.

You have just memorized that list of ten unrelated objects. I know what you're thinking. Hurry up and ask me before I forget. You may be wondering, *"How will I ever hold on to all that."* The answer is, you don't have to. You have placed that sequence in a particular place in your mind, and you know where to go to retrieve it. You have locked them in your mind.

Let's try it. Picture the book. Think of what came next. Picture that and see what came next. Keep going until you have repeated the whole list. How did you do? Pretty well, I would imagine. Chances are, each image you recalled presented your conscious mind with the other image that was linked to it. If you did miss one or two go back over the descriptions of images and then try again. This is a new concept and it may take a couple tries.

Each image acted like a magnet pointing you to the part of the brain where the next image was stored.

That was really quite a fancy bit of memorizing. You saw those objects once, then committed them to memory in order. In fact, you know the order backward as well as forward. Try it. What was the last item? When you picture it what do you see? Now follow the trail back to the first item. Amazing isn't it?

So you see, the mind really is capable of memorizing quickly and efficiently. But, how does it work?

Our basic principal is that **whenever two items are pictured in a silly, painful, or embarrassing association, the thought of one automatically brings the other to mind as though the two are linked.**

Picturing the items to be remembered is very important. We respond more naturally to images than we do to words. We always check out what is in our field of vision. Therefore, whatever we want to remember should be pictured. In fact, the more vivid the picture the more readily we'll remember it.

Silly, painful or embarrassing pictures stand out more than others do. Therefore, they are more powerful at springing back to mind.

We picture two items together so that one reminds us of the next. That way, the most we ever have to keep in mind at any time is two objects. Two is the easiest number of items to remember. We use only two items per picture so that we don't get confused about the order of the items.

In order to leave a path for the memory to follow; we must associate facts to other links in the mind. There are many ways of doing this, depending upon the type of information to be memorized. The one we just did used each object that was memorized as the link for finding the next one.

This approach is called the **linking system**. The objects are linked together like the cars on a train. Each one is linked to the one in front of it and the one behind it. We can follow the train from one car to the next, forward or backward.

That's a neat trick, but what does it do for you? Soon we will see how to apply the linking system to real learning tasks.

IMAGERY: THE MAGIC WAND OF MEMORY

The ability to conjure up pictures in the mind is the magic wand of memory skills. This one skill makes all things possible. Time spent practicing imagery makes you a mental wizard.

We all form images naturally. It's the way our brains work. Our minds do their thinking in images. We only communicate with each other in words. At any waking moment there is a stream of pictures going through our minds. Some will command our attention; others are seen only by the subconscious.

The magic is in consciously building those images. The images we purposely design are much easier to recall than those merely floating on our stream of consciousness.

It may seem awkward at first. With practice, however, you will quickly become skilled at making strong images:

Here's a reminder:

Your image doesn't need to represent the concept, only remind you of it. The ability to bring the information back to mind is all that's important.

The image can be of the most tenuous relationship. It might not make sense to anyone else. For instance, your image for "viaduct" might be Groucho Marks because of his famous comedy routine. If seeing Groucho brings "viaduct" to mind, then it is a wonderful image. It is just as good as, or better than, an architecturally correct image of a viaduct.

Keep it simple

There are a number of mental disciplines that employ imagery. In mental relaxation one creates complex images of their favorite place. It may be a verdant meadow, lush with greenery, filled with sound of rippling water cascading through the rocky stream. Deer play on the field and birds drift lazily in the sky above.

That is far too much work for what we are doing here. In mnemonics we want simple, easily visualized images. They should not require a lot of layering, just a quick glance of the mind's eye. If you think of a meadow, just see a meadow.

Variety is the spice of life

There are many ways to see the same thing. If I asked you to visualize a card, some people would see a playing card. Some would see a credit card. Others would see a business card or a card of wool. To become good at quickly generating images, practice thinking of several images for the same concept.

Exercise: Stop for a minute and write down as many images as you can think of for "horse."

How many did you get? If you answered ten or more you are doing well. If you got 25 you will soon have a great memory. What were your images? Did you see several types of horse? Thoroughbred, Appaloosa, Palomino, Clydesdale? Did you also see a sawhorse? A seahorse? A gymnastics horse? A hoarse throat? Shooting basketballs? There are literally hundreds of possibilities.

It becomes more difficult when you try to form an image for an abstract concept. Words like "duty," "philosophy" or "fortitude" are soft thoughts, difficult to mold into hard images. So use a little magic.

Sounds Like

Again, the image does not have to perfectly represent the concept. It only has to remind you of it. Therefore, <u>porpoise</u> makes a good image for "purpose." <u>Tooth</u> may work for "truth. " "Indemnity" can become <u>a denim tee</u>.

The power of the pun

Never underestimate the power of the pun. Even though the pun is a lower form of humor, more likely to get a groan than a laugh, it is still a powerful memory aid.

There is an old song about the states that is all puns. "How did <u>Wiscon sin</u>? She stole a <u>new brass key</u>." These puns are great images for the states.

If you were linking the capitals to the states, you could picture Wiscon sinning on Madison Avenue. You would then remember that Madison is the capital of Wisconsin. If you pictured <u>linking</u> two new brass keys, you would remember that Lincoln is the capital of Nebraska. Puns are natural mnemonics. Have fun with them.

The first shall be best

Assume you are trying to come up with an image for a concept. Whatever springs into your mind first is most likely to come to mind when you are trying to recall it. If the first image reminds you of the item, go with it.

Recycle

Images that work once will work again. In fact, the more often you use them the better they work. If you use porpoise every time you want to remember purpose, you don't have to stop and think of an image; it's there. When you recall it you know exactly what it means.

When you have used mnemonics for a while you will find that you have an inventory of images. They act like a magic wand to make all sorts of information reappear in your mind, as if by magic.

APPLYING THE LINKING METHOD

The linking system preserves information in the order in which it is learned. To retrieve the material you start at one end of the chain and proceed to the other. This arrangement is easily adapted to memorizing lectures or presentations. It could be used equally well to give a presentation as to study one.

As an example, let's assume we're studying American History. In particular, we are studying about Andrew Jackson.

Read the following material and then let's memorize some key issues of Andrew Jackson's administration:

> We learn that Jackson used the spoils system. He handed out high level patronage jobs to those who helped him get elected. Some of these people even held cabinet posts (for which they were ill prepared.)

> In order to stay abreast of issues, Jackson had a group of unofficial advisers to whom he actually listened. Though they had no cabinet posts or official positions, they did, however, know their fields well. The press began to call this group the "Kitchen Cabinet."

> Jackson also made our democracy more democratic. He made judges and constables elected positions, and required caucuses for the nomination of candidates in the Democratic Party.

> A very contentious issue of Jackson's administration was the "Tariff of Abominations." The northern majority in congress passed this tariff which called for very high tariffs on manufactured goods from abroad. The southern states wanted low tariffs, while the north wanted the high tariffs to protect their manufacturing.

South Carolina passed a law nullifying the tariff in their state. They then refused to collect custom duties. Furthermore, they threatened to secede from the Union if forced to comply with the tariff.

In response, Jackson got legislation from Congress called the "Force Act" which gave him the power to send federal troops to enforce the Union. There was little doubt in anyone's mind that he would use these powers.

The matter was resolved, not by war, but by the "Compromise of 1832." This compact reduced the tariffs gradually over a period of 10 years.

To memorize all of that, you merely need a picture for each issue. The pictures can then be linked together to lock the chain of events in your memory.

You can use the images in the table below. The issues are in the left-hand column. Suggested images are in the right. Picture the images in successive pairs, just as we did before.

Andrew Jackson	CAR JACK
The spoils system	GARBAGE
His kitchen cabinet	KITCHEN CABINET
Improving democracy	DONKEY
Tariff of abominations	ABOMINABLE SNOWMAN
Secede	SEED (Sounds like secede.)
Force act	HAMMER
Compromise of 1832	HANDSHAKE

Picture a car jack for Jackson. Now picture yourself using the jack to raise a pile of garbage. This symbolizes "spoils system."

Next, visualize the garbage in your kitchen cabinet.

Then imagine a donkey, for democracy, in your kitchen cabinet.

Visualize the Abominable Snowman riding the poor little donkey.

Then see the snowman growing out of a large seed (sounds like secede.)

Now, mentally smash that seed with a hammer. (For force)

Next, visualize yourself shaking hands (the compromise) with a swinging hammer.

Now, close the book and recall the images in order. Notice that with the images come the issues that were memorized and the details we didn't memorize.

The linking system leads the way back to things you wanted to remember.

Go over the list one more time. You now have the notes on Andrew Jackson memorized. Try it. Picture your image for Andrew Jackson, then see what comes next. Follow each image until you reach the end of the notes.

Notice that each image reminds you of a cluster of information, not just the image. That is the wonderful thing about mnemonics. We don't need to memorize every detail. Our linked images have given us a map. It guides us to the places in our mind where the information is stored.

The linking system can be used to memorize notes from a class as easily as it can for written material. If you have taken notes on a class or lecture you attended, look through the notes. For each paragraph or cluster of ideas, choose one image to remind you of the main idea. It doesn't have to represent the idea, only remind you of it. When you have an image for each of the groups of ideas, link them together. This is the same thing we did with the material on Andrew Jackson.

Next, repeat the list of images a few times and you will easily remember all of your notes on the subject.

You might think of the linking system as the spool of string that cave-explorers carry on their backs. The string is fastened at the opening of the cave and played out as the explorer goes in. No matter which turns the spelunker takes; the string shows the way back. The linking system is like that. You can return to where you were in your brain by following the linked images. Once you get there you can look and see what's there.

VOCABULARY

Memorizing vocabulary is one important application of the linking system. We are frequently faced with having to learn new terms and their meanings. When we take on a new job there are new processes, names, equipment and systems. When we take a class, lots of new terminology is always involved. Traveling in foreign countries or dealing with people who do not speak our language makes it necessary to add new words and phrases to our vocabulary quickly. The process for memorizing vocabulary is the same as the normal **linking method** but there are only two items in each chain.

Naming the plates

When my wife and I were young and newly married we backpacked around Europe. Each country we visited presented new joys and new challenges. There were train schedules to learn, money to convert, and new foods to try. But, the most immediate challenge was the language.

Life in a foreign country can be very trying if you don't know how to order from a menu, or find a hotel. You can easily be cheated if you don't know the numbers or currencies. And there is a very special frustration in not knowing which rest room is which.

As we entered each country on the train, I would memorize a basic survival vocabulary from a phrase book. One German phrase I remember well is **"Nehmen sie platz, bitte."** It means, "Please sit down."

I did not expect to ever use it, but it was easy to remember. One night we were sitting in a club with another American couple when a group of German men came in. We were at a large table but there were only four of us. Seeing a chance to use my phrase, I said, **"Nehmen sie platz, bitte."** The men smiled and sat down.

What they said next, I haven't a clue. They assumed we knew the language. It took a while, but we did get to know each other. Among the two groups we had some languages in common.

We ended up spending the evening together and having a great time. We really enjoyed each other's company and learned a lot in the process. Without that phrase, however, I doubt we would have ever met.

Learning a language is a long and demanding process. Learning new vocabulary, however, can be fairly easy. The same basic principle of mnemonics applies. Whenever two objects are pictured in a silly, illogical, painful or ridiculous association, the thought of one recalls the other.

In this case, the two items associated are the word and the meaning. Consider the phrase above: **"Nehmen sie platz, bitte."** We can picture the meaning; someone sitting down. How do we picture the words, though? The simplest technique is to make up a phrase that sounds like the phrase. In this case, I pictured 'Naming the plates bitterly' for **"Nehmen sie platz, bitte."** After a few repetitions it is a known phrase.

To associate the two together I pictured someone sitting on the plates as they were named.

The same approach works with any word or name. The following are some French words and their meanings. Next to each meaning is an image that can be used to remember it.

ENGLISH	FRENCH	PRONUN-CIATION	IMAGE
Man	Homme	Awm	A man taking *Alms*.
Lady	Dame	Dahm	A woman in a *dome*.
Waiter	garcon	Gar saun	Waiter singing a *car song*.
Elevator	Ascenseur	Ah soun sur	*A censor* in the elevator.
hot	Chaude	Showed	Hot water in the spotlight. (*Showed*)

Go over the list a couple times. Picture the image for each word. Don't just read it or say it. The trick is to establish the image, which will recall the meaning. Now cover the table above and write the English words for the French words below.

FRENCH	ENGLISH
Homme	
Dame	
Garcon	
Ascenseur	
Chaude	

How did you do? Were you able to conjure up the images? Did the meanings come to mind? Chances are it took a little time. With a few repetitions, that time would shrink to almost none. Let's try it the other way.

At this time cover the above tables. Now try the same thing given the English word. Picture the image for the word and an image for the French equivalent should come to mind.

ENGLISH	FRENCH
Man	
Lady	
Waiter	
Elevator	
Hot	
Necktie	

Was that any easier? It usually is less difficult to go from our own language to the other. With repetition this simple technique will help you to remember vocabulary easily. Later you will see how putting these images on the hook system will multiply the number of words you can quickly learn.

SUMMARY

For practical purposes there is no limit to the amount of information we can retain in our memories. Where we have difficulty is finding the specific fact or item that we need.

The science of mnemonics is a way of organizing and navigating the material we put in our memories. It is a way of marking information as we put it into the mind so that we can locate it quickly when we need it.

The basic principle of our mnemonic system is: **"Whenever two items are pictured in a silly, painful, or embarrassing association, the thought of one automatically brings the other to mind."**

That principle can be remembered in 5 easy steps that spell out the word **SPEAR.**

> **Simplify**
>
> **Picture**
>
> **Embellish**
>
> **Associate**
>
> **Recall**

Simplify the material.

Use only two items per association. Two is the simplest number of things to remember.

Picture each item.

Use any image that will remind you of the item. It can be a pun or something that sounds like the item. It can be a symbol of the item, or it can be the item itself.

Embellish the pictures.

Make the image stand out. Make it too large or small. Make it illogical, painful or emotional. The more outlandish the better.

Associate the items in pairs.

Associate the image for the item with the image for its meaning or significance.

Recall the images.

Repeat the pictures in your mind a few times to strengthen the memory.

We looked at a simple but effective way of applying this principle in the linking method. By associating the first object on a list to the next object on the list we linked them together in our minds. Then we associated the third object with the second, the fourth with the third, and so on.

This gave us the ability to start with either the first or last object on the list and remember each succeeding object in order.

It is quite simple to apply the linking method to memorizing notes. We treat each major idea or heading as an object, create an image for it and associate it with the image that came before it. This builds a chain of images that we can follow from beginning to end.

Exercises

The following exercises are designed to give you practice at using the secret of Linking.

The best exercise is the one you find in daily life. It could be material from a class you are taking, a project you are working on, or anything you are interested in.

LINKING

Linking Exercise 1

Memorize the first thirteen states of the United States in the order that they became states. Form an image to remind you of each state and link them together. You can write your images in the columns below. Try to form your own images first. If you have real difficulty forming one or more of the images, there are some suggestions in the appendix.

STATE	IMAGE FOR STATE	CONNECTION
Delaware		
Pennsylvania		
New Jersey		
Georgia		
Connecticut		
Massachusetts		
Maryland		
South Carolina		
New Hampshire		
Virginia		
New York		
North Carolina		
Rhode Island		

Linking Exercise 2

Memorize the eleven Confederate States.

STATE	IMAGE FOR STATE	CONNECTION
Alabama		
Arkansas		
Florida		
Georgia		
Louisiana		
Mississippi		
North Carolina		
South Carolina		
Tennessee		
Texas		
Virginia		

Linking Exercise 3

Memorize the ages of the earth.

AGES OF THE EARTH	IMAGE FOR AGE	CONNECTION
Pre Cambrian		
Cambrian		
Ordovician		
Silurian		
Devonian		
Pennsylvanian		
Permian		
Triassic		
Jurassic		
Cretaceous		
Tertiary		
Quaternary		

Linking Exercise 4

Memorize the ranking of hands in Poker.

HAND	IMAGE	CONNECTION
Straight Flush		
Four of a kind		
Full House		
Flush		
Straight		
Three of a kind		
Two pairs		
Pair		
No Pair		

Vocabulary Exercise 1

Memorize the classifications of Taxonomy from General to specific.

CLASSIFICATION	IMAGE	CONNECTION
Kingdom		
Phylum		
Class		
Order		
Family		
Genus		
Species		
Variation		

Vocabulary Exercise 2

Memorize the definitions of the motions of the earth.

MOTION	IMAGE	MEANING	IMAGE
Rotation		The earth spinning on its axis each day.	
Revolution		The movement of the earth around the sun each year.	
Precession		The circular motion of the axis, every 26,000 years. (like a spinning top.)	
Nutation		The slight wobble of the axis within its precession. (Every 19 years.)	
Solar drift		The sun bobs up and down in the galaxy.	
Galactic rotation		The whole galaxy rotates around its common center.	

Vocabulary Exercise 3

Memorize the following phrases in Japanese. (Phonetic spelling).

PHRASE	IMAGE	MEANING	CONNECTION
O-ha-yo		Good Morning	
Ko-nee-chee-wa		Good Afternoon	
Kohn-bahn-wa		Good Evening	
Sa-yo-na-ra		Goodbye	
Do-zo		Please	
Ah-ree-ga-toh		Thank you	
Doh-ee-ta-shee-ma-shee-the		You're welcome	
Hai		Yes	
Ee-yeh		No	

***

SECRET **3**

**Remembering
What We Read**

SECRET 3
Remembering What We Read

(IT'S IN THE CARDS)

Wouldn't it be wonderful to remember all that we read? Imagine reading a chapter and having the whole thing in your head. You could learn so much more. There is a way to do that and it works like magic.

Just as the magician makes fans of cards appear at his fingertips, you can make the pages of your book appear in your mind. With practice you'll be able to pull the facts out of thin air just like the magician's cards. It's all in the CARDS.

Let's look first at a method to increase our normal retention. This technique will enhance our total learning. Then we'll learn how to commit what we read to memory.

The CARDS method of reading for comprehension

Reading for retention is most successful when you plan the event. Follow the steps below and you will find your comprehension growing with each new article or chapter you read.

Consider
Ask
Read
Describe &
Study

*C*onsider the material.

Look at the structure of the chapter or article before you actually read it. If there is an outline, read it. If not, make your own out of section headings; bold face words, or even lead sentences if necessary. Always look at the charts, pictures and tables before reading the material.

By considering the material you will know the design and thrust of it. This is how you stack the deck in your favor. When it comes time to do the reading it will be familiar to you.

*A*sk Questions:

Once the outline is known it is time to ask the golden question.

"What do I want out of this reading?" The answer to that question gives you a clear objective for your learning task. (You may learn at this point that it does not fit your interests or is not worthy of further consideration.)

Also, if there are any questions to be answered at the end of the chapter or in a workbook, read them now. Knowing what the questions are helps you recognize the answers. An unanswered question puts the mind on edge. It creates what psychologists call a cognitive dissonance. Your mind hungrily looks for the answer to relieve the dissonance.

*R*ead the material:

Now read the material with the objective in mind. You already have a clear sense of the structure and meaning of the article or chapter. You also know what the questions are.

You are prepared to learn. Like a card shark, you have sized up the situation and are ready to play.

Describe the material:

Having read it, tell yourself what you have learned.

You should be able to simply state the basic points and the tone of the material. This step focuses the mind on what it has just absorbed. It helps to put the material in order in your memory.

Study:

Now answer any questions about the material. Having read the questions ahead of time the answers should be apparent now.

Next, follow the outline to see if you have retained the main ideas. Look up any items you may have missed. Use a dictionary to look up any terms that weren't clear to you.

This structured approach to remembering what you read will yield much better retention than the normal method of just reading it and writing notes.

Exercise:

Find an article in a periodical, on the Internet, or a textbook that you would like to read. Plan your learning of the article. Follow the steps outlined above and read the article.

Remember that it's in the CARDS.

Consider the article:

Go over any outline, charts, pictures, or headings.

Ask questions about the article:

What do you want to learn from the article? What questions were posed by your consideration of the article?

Read the article.

Describe what you learned.

Study the article.

Did it answer your questions?

After you finish reading the article this way, assess your retention. If you can state the main points of the article and how they relate, you have done a good job.

WHEN THE STAKES ARE HIGH

Sometimes there is more on the line than just knowing the material. Maybe this is for the big test. Maybe there is a promotion on the line. Perhaps you are trying to come up to speed on a new job and you want to know the material with dead certainty. Here is where your memory system pays you back for all your practice.

Only one extra step is needed to cement this reading material into your mind in exquisite detail. That is to memorize the outline.

Remember that the formula is to Consider, Ask, Read, Describe and Study. Now, during the **"Consider"** phase, memorize the outline that you developed.

There are several methods available for memorizing outlines. One of the best is the Landmark method. Following the next chapter there is an exercise that will lead you through memorizing what you read.

***

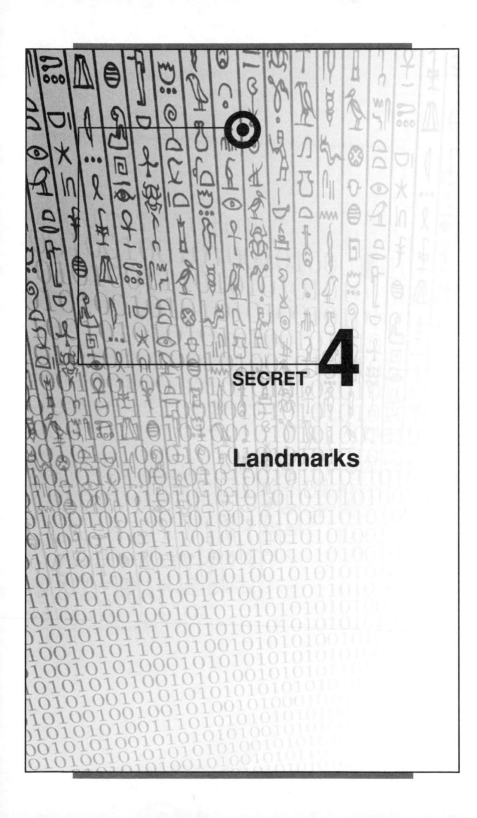

SECRET **4**

Landmarks

SECRET 4
Landmarks

Without consciously realizing it, we each have a whole universe of landmarks in the small confines of our mind.

Think of a place, one of your favorite places. Picture it in detail. See where it is, what's close to it, what is in it, what are the colors, the shapes, the feelings of the place.

How difficult was it to find that place? How easily could you picture details? It was probably a very simple task. That place is a landmark, a place in the mind that you can go to without really thinking about it. That place is as easy to find as your way home.

We tend to have a great facility for imagining, and therefore, remembering places. This makes life much more pleasant, as well as safer. We need to remember places well just to get around. That's why we're good at it.

This facility, remembering places, seems to be built into all animals that roam. Even some of the nature's smallest creatures possess it. Take the chickadee, for instance. This shy and diminutive bird gathers and stores seeds. It puts them in various hiding places in its range. Tests have shown that the chickadee can still remember where it hid seeds up to 2 weeks after hiding them.

51

The Monarch butterfly migrates each year to a specific grove of trees in Mexico. Many of these small insects fly all the way from Canada. A journey of more than a thousand miles is an awesome feat for anyone. But, here is an animal with a brain weighing less than a gram. That tiny brain has such a strong sense of landmarks, though, that it can traverse a continent and arrive at a precise destination.

Compared to the chickadee and the monarch, we have massive brains. Our capacity for remembering places is correspondingly immense. We can picture every nook and cranny of our homes, every portion of our route to work or school. We can also remember other homes and buildings we've seen or visited.

We are very well suited to remember landmarks. This is something the mind is good at remembering. Let's use it to remember other things, which are not so easily remembered.

Try it first and see how easy it is. There are ten objects listed below.

Pineapple
Mouse
Book
Boat
Flashlight
Hat
Cow
Chessboard
Fire
Telephone

Now, look around the room you are in right now. Pick out little landmarks in the room. Picture each one of these objects on one of those landmarks. You might picture the pineapple on a desk or in a drawer or on the ceiling. When you have pictured each object in a place, close the book and mentally return to your landmarks.

Do you remember what you saw in each place? If you missed a couple, look at the list and see what it was. Now close the book and try again. This time should do it.

When we recall a landmark we easily remember what was there. This is basic to our survival. If we didn't recall where we were, we would never get home. If we didn't remember where to get food and water, we would be in real trouble. Without a memory of dangerous places we would get hurt more often. Mental processes that we need to survive tend to be very well developed. That's why they make such great memory aids.

There is one other thing that makes landmarks an excellent platform for memorizing. The places in our mind are already organized. Each room, or street, or piece of furniture that we can picture has an orderly set of parts or sub-places. This allows us to fit the organization of the information to the organization of the places. The very structure of the places can tell us about the information.

Let's assume you are memorizing information about the planets of our solar system and using your house as a set of landmarks. You might picture a big thermometer in the basement to remind you of Mercury. You could use the furnace as a landmark within the basement. Mercury is a planet that is cold on one side and very hot on the other because it rotates about as fast as it revolves. If you picture the furnace glowing red hot on one side and covered with ice on the other, you will remember that.

The fact that it is on the furnace in the basement tells you that that fact relates to Mercury, not another planet. Mercury is in the basement.

The following is a form you can use for setting up a Landmark system for anything you wish to memorize. You simply write what you wish to remember in the first column, the place you will remember it in the second column, and the image for the item in the third. For instance, using your house as a set of landmarks to memorize the planets, you would write Mercury in the first column. In the second column write basement. Put thermometer in the third column.

Similarly, you would put Venus in the first column, kitchen in the second column and the statue of Venus in the third column. When you had all nine planets and their assigned landmarks down, you would review the list. The form helps you to organize your landmarks and is a quick reference if you forget one or two items.

Copy the form so that you can use it over and over. Later we'll practice using this same form to memorize what we read later in the book.

SUBJECT:_____
Room:_____

ITEM	LANDMARK	IMAGE

Landmarks Exercise 1

Use the **Landmarks** technique to memorize the following outline. Use the **CARDS** technique to remember what you read. Follow the instructions below. Do not read the article until you memorize the outline.

GLACIERS

TYPES OF GLACIERS

Ice shelf

Valley glacier

Piedmont glacier

Outlet glacier

SURFACE FEATURES

Moraine

Crevasses

Glacier Table

The charts that follow the article offer an effective way to use the Landmark system. The items to be memorized are listed in three columns. The first column contains the item itself. The middle column holds the landmark where it will be remembered. The third column has the image for the item. This format is easy to prepare and neatly organizes the material. You would normally write it out but here it is written out for you.

GLACIERS

ITEM	PLACE	IMAGE
GLACIERS	LIVING ROOM	GLACIER
Types of Glaciers	Couch	Typewriter
Surface Features	Stereo	Glacier Surface

INSTRUCTIONS

You will want to organize the outline in levels. So start by memorizing your major headings.

First, picture a glacier in your living room. The room is full of snowy ice.

Now, imagine a huge typewriter on your couch. This will symbolize types of glaciers.

Next, picture the surface of the glacier on top of your stereo. This will represent surface features of glaciers.

TYPES OF GLACIERS [COUCH]

ITEM	PLACE	IMAGE
Ice sheet	Cushion	Frozen sheet
Ice Shelf	Back	Icy shelf
Valley	Leg	Valley
Piedmont	Arm	Mountain of peas
Outlet	Webbing	Electrical outlet

INSTRUCTIONS

Now, move down a level in organization. Picture the different types of glaciers on parts of the couch.

Picture a cushion of the couch wrapped in a frozen, icy sheet. **(Ice sheet)**

Then image a shelf made out of solid ice attached to the back of the couch. **(Ice shelf)**

Now visualize that the leg of the couch is standing in a valley. **(Valley glacier)**

On the arm of the couch picture a mountain of peas. **(Piedmont glacier)**

In the webbing under the cushion, picture an electrical outlet. **(Outlet glacier)**

SURFACE FEATURES

[Stereo]

ITEM	PLACE	IMAGE
Moraine	CD Player	More rain
Crevasses	Tape Deck	Crayfish
Glacier table	Phonograph	Table of ice

INSTRUCTIONS

We'll now do the same thing for Surface Features. This heading is on the stereo, so we will picture the subheadings on parts of the stereo.

See 'more rain' on the CD player. Everything is getting wet. (Moraine)

Now picture 'crayfish' in the tape deck. (Crevasse)

Finally, imagine a table of ice on the phonograph. (Glacier table)

At this point the outline exists in your mind in a very organized manner. The headings are on different pieces of furniture. Subheadings are on parts of those pieces of furniture.

Once you have memorized the outline, ask your questions of the material and then read the article on glaciers.

Do not try to memorize while you are reading. This is very difficult and not at all practical. If you memorize the outline, it will keep the text of the article or chapter in place in your mind.

At the end of the reading, describe what you have learned. You should be able to go around the furniture in your living room and recall the major headings from the outline.

Repeat your mental tour of the living room a couple of times. Practice makes perfect.

Now, read the article on the next page.

GLACIERS

A glacier is a large mass of mobile, permanent ice formed on land by the compaction of snow. It may move down a slope by gravity, or fan out because of its own thickness. Glaciers may stop on land or move out onto the ocean, or a lake.

They may be smaller than a mile long or they may grow to immense continent size proportions. The great Antarctica ice sheet covers 4,826,000 square miles. All of the great mountain ranges have glaciers. Indeed, glaciers store about 75 percent of the Earth's fresh water.

TYPE OF GLACIERS

An ice sheet is a dome-shaped glacier covering an area of more than 19,300 square miles. It moves outward in all directions. Because of its size the landscape does not impede its movement. The Antarctic and Greenland ice sheets are the only ones still in existence. In the Pleistocene Epoch, ice sheets covered the northern parts of both North America and Europe.

About 90 percent of the world's glacial ice is in the Antarctic ice sheet. It is more than 50% larger than the contiguous United States. If the Antarctic ice sheet were to melt completely, sea level around the world would rise more than 200 ft. Most coastal cities would be under water.

The lowest air temperature ever recorded anywhere was -128.6° F. at the Vostok Station on the Antarctic ice sheet. The snowfall in the central part of the ice sheet is less than

2 inches per year. This central part of the ice sheet is therefore as dry as a desert.

Though the ice sheet is currently shrinking, the Earth's crust has been depressed by the great weight of the Antarctic ice sheet. The great depth of the Antarctic continental shelf resulted from this depression.

The Greenland ice sheet is smaller and the climate is less rigorous.

An **ice shelf** is a thick, flat, floating sheet of ice. It is attached to the land on one or more sides and floats in the ocean. The leading edge ends in a vertical ice cliff, as much as 100 ft high. Many of the huge icebergs break off of these ice shelves.

An alpine, mountain, or **valley glacier** flows down a valley. Tens of thousands of them exist at the present time. They are built by snow and restrained by the walls of the valleys. This causes them to be much longer than they are wide. Some are less than a half mile long. One in Alaska is over 68 miles in length.

The point where a valley glacier leaves its valley and spreads out over the foothills and plains is called a **piedmont glacier**. Two or more valley glaciers meeting and extending beyond the valley walls form the largest ones.

Outlet glaciers extend from the edge of an ice sheet or ice cap into a preexisting valley. Tidewater glaciers, found only in rugged coastal regions of high latitudes, are sources of icebergs.

SURFACE FEATURES

A moraine is a surface ridge of material near the middle of a glacier. It is aligned parallel to the flow lines of the glacier and moves down a valley with it. A trunk glacier formed from a number of tributary flows will usually have as many moraines on it as it has tributary glaciers.

Crevasses, wedge-shaped cracks or fissures in the surface of an ice sheet or glacier, are formed by stresses set up by ice movement. Some crevasses can grow to over 70 feet wide and hundreds of yards long. In winter they are often hidden by snow bridges, making travel dangerous.

A glacier table is a large block of stone resting on an ice pedestal, which may rise 10 feet or more above the surface of a glacier. A glacier table is formed when the stone is large enough to insulate the ice immediately beneath it from the sun's radiation. The pedestal gets higher as the surface of the glacier is lowered by ablation.

The end

Now, think back to the outline you memorized earlier. Go around your living room and see what you pictured there. As you mentally look at each landmark, your mind will see the thing you pictured there. This allows you to describe the whole article by following the outline in your head. That, my friend, is excellent retention.

A MILLION PLACES

Any setting can be used for Landmarks. If you have used your living room you can then use your kitchen, bedroom, or basement. An average home has thousands of easily recalled places in it.

Your home can be used over and over again. If you do have an active body of information in your home now, use your office, or your car, or your parents' home. Other possibilities are your car, clothes, route to work or school, your church, or any place you know well.

Most people use the same places over and over again. The more familiar they are the better they work. The trick is to use the system often. Practice makes perfect. This skill can serve for years to come.

Exercise Landmarks 1

Memorize the Families of Shorebirds using your kitchen.

SHORE BIRDS		
ITEM	**PLACE**	**IMAGE**
Shore birds	Kitchen	
Plovers		
Oystercatchers		
Stilts		
Jacanas		
Sandpipers		
Turnstones		
Surfbirds		
Phalaropes		
Gulls		
Jaegers		
Gulls		
Terns		
Skimmers		
Alcids		

***

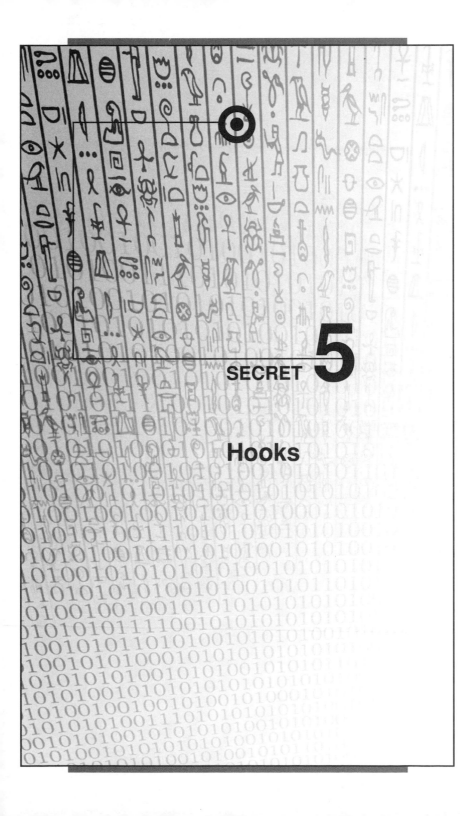

SECRET **5**

Hooks

SECRET 5
Hooks

The linking method is very useful for learning long lists, classes, speeches, etc. in their exact order. Sometimes, however, the position of items on a list is very important and we don't want to repeat a whole list just to recall one item. There is a system by which we can place individual facts in their respective places and recall them separately. It's called the hook system.

Imagine going to a party in wintertime in someone's home. Because of the limited closet space, you end up putting coats on the host's bed. Then, when it's time to leave, you have to root through all the coats to find yours. The system works for the small party.

When you go to an event at a large hotel, though, they don't have you take your coats and hats up and put them on the beds. They use a coat check. The attendant puts your coat on a specific hook and gives you a tag that tells the number of that hook.

When you return for your wrap, you give that person the tag and a tip, and they will go to the specific hook and retrieve your coat and hat. It's a very orderly system.

We can organize our memories the same way by building a set of mental hooks. Our basic principle says that,

"Whenever two items are pictured together in a silly, illogical, painful, or ridiculous association, the thought of one automatically brings the other to mind."

We all know the numbers from one to 10. If we memorize concrete images for each of the numbers, it will give us a set of clearly numbered hooks just like those in the coat check. Then, when we associate something with the image for a given number, it not only tells us what it is, but also, where it is.

An easy way of memorizing hooks is to assign a word to each number that rhymes with it, sounds like it, or in some way reminds us of it. For instance, the image for four may be a golfer yelling "FORE." Or, it might be "FLOOR", or it might be "WIND" for the four winds. Any easily remembered image will work.

Here is a list of hooks that are easy to commit to memory. Practice recalling them until the images and numbers will be interchangeable.

One	Wand	**Six**	Chicks
Two	Shoe	**Seven**	Heaven
Three	Tree	**Eight**	Gate
Four	Floor	**Nine**	Pine
Five	Hive	**Ten**	Pen

If there is something that comes to mind more readily than one of these hooks, by all means use it. In fact, replace any hook that doesn't work very well for you with one that is easily remembered.

To use the hooks, merely associate each new fact with the image for the number. When you need to know what is number 6 on your list, just visualize your image for six and you will see what you associated with it. Conversely, if you want to know where something fits on the list, think of the item and you will recall the image of the number. It's a very efficient system.

This system is so powerful; you don't even need to learn the items in order. You merely have to associate them with the right hook and you will be able to put them in order in your head. In a minute we will try it. Before we begin, however, stop and review your hooks. Recite the words for the numbers one through ten.

How did you do? If you missed some, try again. Go back and look them up.

Now, let's use our hooks to memorize the first ten presidents of the United States. In fact, to prove a point, we'll learn them out of order and remember them in order. I'll assume that we are using the hooks we just learned. If you have a different hook for a given number, use that. If a better image springs to mind, by all means use that.

THE PRESIDENTS

Starting with number one, picture a "wand," like a magic wand. George Washington was the first president. What

71

image would work for Washington? He chopped down the cherry tree, so picture **George chopping that cherry tree with a wand**. It doesn't cut very well at all.

Let's jump to number nine. The hook for nine is "pine," so picture a pinecone. The ninth president was Harrison. Hair would remind us of Harrison so **picture the pinecone covered with hair.**

Move on now to number four. Here the hook is floor. Picture the floor where you are now. The fourth president was Madison. We could think of Madison Square Gardens for Madison. Picture lots of **square gardens on the floor** where you are right now. That should bring back Madison.

The hook for ten was "hen." The president was Tyler. Imagine a **pen writing all over the tile**.

The fifth president is Monroe. The hook for five is "hive." You might picture **Marilyn Monroe with a beehive in her blonde hair**.

Number eight is "gate." The eighth president was VanBuren. If we look for something that sounds like VanBuren we might think of a van burning. Picture **a burning van crashing through the gate.**

The third president was Jefferson. The hook for three is "tree." Jefferson is on the two-dollar bill and on the nickel. We could imagine **a tree growing two-dollar bills in great abundance.** That should remind us of Jefferson.

The sixth hook is "chicks." The sixth president was John Quincy Adams. We could picture **chicks with big adam's apples**.

Seven is "heaven." The seventh president is Andrew Jackson. We already have an image for Jackson. Remember, it was a "car jack." We could picture **someone using a car jack to try and lift heaven**.

Finally, the second president was John Adams. The hook for two is "shoe." We already have an image for Adams. It is adam's apple. Just picture **being kicked in on your adam's apple by a shoe**.

Now go back up to where it says 'The Presidents' and go over that list again one more time.

Okay, think of what has transpired. You have memorized the ten presidents. You learned the information out of order and now you will put it back into order in your mind. This is a truly remarkable bit of memorizing. Now, picture your hooks in order and name the presidents that they call to mind.

This method of memorizing is very powerful. With practice you can commit volumes of information to memory and use it instantaneously.

How much material can one hook hold?

Think of the hook for seven. Who is the president that we have memorized there?

What do we know about Jackson? He used the spoils system. He had a kitchen cabinet. He made the democracy more democratic, etc.

By combining the linking method with the hooks, we can memorize a great deal on a simple set of hooks. Imagine that you have memorized information about each of the first ten presidents of the United States. Now, by recalling the hook for each president you could bring forth the history of each administration. All of this information is very neatly organized in your memory.

Now you would have a much better understanding of this early period in American history. You could compare the actions of individual presidents in similar circumstances. The philosophical differences between Monroe and Jefferson would be clear in your mind. You would know how Jackson responded to economic conditions and how that compared to Tyler's response.

The combination of the two memory systems is an extremely potent learning tool.

How many hooks is enough?

The more hooks you can command, the stronger your memory gets. This is true up to a point. Most people who use hooks regularly find that 100 hooks will fill most of their needs.

Add to your list of hooks as time goes by. Learning the number system will help with this. If you add a few each week you will soon be up to 100. The larger your set of working hooks the larger your mental capacity.

VARIOUS WAYS TO MAKE HOOKS

From the mouths of babes:

When our children were little we used to read to them in the evenings. From the delightful word play of Dr. Seuss to the clever poetry of Shel Silverstien they loved to hear their favorite books over and over again.

When he was two or three, Sean was especially fond of one particular pop-up book. This was a book of the alphabet. There was a pop-up, slide or picture for every single letter. Like all children, Sean learned his alphabet by singing a little song. He knew the order of the letters by rhythm, but he learned the shape and sound of the letters by means of this pop-up book.

After we read this book an inordinate number of times, (sometimes twice a night) Sean knew what was coming next. He was quite proud to tell me the letter and what animal or symbol was on the next page.

It soon occurred to me, that he had a very good set of hooks. He knew the order of the letters and had a visual image for each one. We began to play a game with the characters. I would say, "Let's pretend the alligator has a balloon in his mouth." Or "Let's pretend the magician is pulling a car out of his hat." We made the images very silly on purpose.

He never missed a beat. He knew where everything was. When I would ask "Where is the balloon or what is in the magician's hat," he knew. We played this game a lot.

I have tried this with other children as well, and the result is the same. If they know a sequence they can readily use it as hooks. Sometimes it's a song they sang at home or at church.

"This old man, he played two, he played knick-knack on his shoe....." would yield shoe for two. Sometimes it's the pictures on the alphabet blocks they play with. Any known system works.

So, if you remember your alphabet or number book from childhood, or you remember your child's, that is a set of hooks you already have. It's also a good way to teach children to use hooks. (Just don't tell them you're teaching them something. Let it be a game.)

It's all in how you look at it:

Anyone who plays chess knows what the pieces are. They know the king, queen, rook, etc. The pieces have the same function on any board. The rules are the same all over the world. Though there is only one organization of the chess pieces, there are thousands of styles of chess pieces. There are civil war chess sets, crystal chess sets, roman chess sets, cartoon sets, the Alice in Wonderland chess set, etc. The average chess player can play with any of these sets. He or she will know which piece is the queen and which is the rook.

The same is true of our set of ten hooks. They are: one-wand, two-shoe, three-tree, etc.

But there are many ways to picture a wand or a shoe or a tree.

Supposing you have memorized something on those ten hooks and now you have something else you want to remember. With no effort at all you can double your inventory of hooks.

All you need do is change the picture for the hook. If you pictured a magician's wand for 'one,' picture the wand of a vacuum cleaner this time. If you pictured a dress shoe for number 'two' last time, picture a running shoe this time. Now you have an entirely new set of hooks that work well because you already know their order.

With just the ten basic hooks you could expand your capacity to several times that level. For instance, you could organize them into categories. You could have formal hooks, sports hooks, trashy hooks, fantasy hooks, toy hooks, etc. Whatever your imagination produces will work well for you. Look at the following possibilities:

ORIGINAL	FORMAL	SPORTS	FANTASY
Wand	conductor's wand	bat	wizard's staff
Shoe	tuxedo shoe	track shoe	elf shoe
Tree	tree on an estate	goal post	tree house
Floor	marble floor	gym floor	trap door
Hive	queen bee	sport bees	huge bees
Chicks	peacock chicks	pheasant	dragons
Heaven	golden stairs	racing angels	misty castle in clouds
Gate	courthouse doors	starting gate	time portal
Wine	champagne	Gatorade	magic potion
Pen	fountain pen	marker	quill pen

If you take the time to set up sets of hooks and memorize them you can quickly come up with lots of well-organized hooks.

That Reminds Me:

I have an aunt who is a great conversationalist. She could talk to anyone. Staying on track, however, is not one of her strong suits. She is not a listener. As someone else would start to say something, she would blurt, "Oh! That reminds me! ....," and off she would go on a totally unrelated topic. Keeping up with her takes great concentration.

Aunt Bess just can't seem to save a thought. She has to share whatever comes to mind with whomever will listen. To some extent we all do that. How many times in a day does one thing remind us of another? It's almost constant. That tendency provides us with another way to quickly design new hooks.

If you think about it, each of the hooks reminds you of something else. The beehive may remind us of honey, the pen may remind us of paper. Any image that a hook reminds us of is also a hook. Check out the list below.

HOOK	REMINDER	REMINDER	REMINDER	REMINDER
Wand	top hat	rabbit	tuxedo	cards
Shoe	sock	shoelaces	shoe polish	galoshes
Tree	grass	acorn	bush	bird nest
Floor	rug	dust	boards	baseboard
Hive	honey	bees	honeycomb	house fly
Chicks	eggs	feed	cage	coop
Heaven	angel	harp	cloud	halo

HOOK	REMINDER	REMINDER	REMINDER	REMINDER
Gate	latch	pickets	yard	fence
Wine	bottle	cork	corkscrew	goblet
Pen	ink	paper	cartridge	clip

Now we've learned forty more hooks. That's a five-time expansion in a couple minutes. To lock them in, you should use each set of hooks in rotation. The more you use them the better they will work.

Place your bets:

You will recall that Landmarks were a good way to store information. We easily remember what we put in our imaginary spaces. If we think of each of our hooks as a collection of places, we can expand the amount of material we put on each hook. Any image has places all over it. This is particularly helpful when you are memorizing several things about each item. First look at the list and then we'll see how it works.

HOOK	PLACE	PLACE	PLACE	PLACE	PLACE
Wand	shaft	end	ferrule	inside	under hand
Shoe	sole	eyelet	tongue	seam	heel
Tree	roots	trunk	branch	leaf	holes
Floor	corner	middle	grout	tile	door sill
Hive	attachment	entry	nursery	queens lair	honeycomb
Chicks	beak	wing	tail	claw	feather
Heaven	throne	walls	St. Peter's	seraphim	edge
Gate	wire	lock	hinge	fence post	gap under
Wine	bottleneck	bottom	label	rim	foil
Pen	point	clip	ink chamber	button	barrel

Now you can learn several things about each item you memorize and put them on the same hook. Let's say you were learning about the planets of the solar system. You would memorize them on hooks: WAND_Mercury; SHOE_Venus; TREE_Earth; etc.

Now you could add information on each planet by memorizing it on parts of the hook. Mercury, for instance, has a
locked orbit. You could picture a padlock in orbit around the
shaft of the wand. Mercury is heavily cratered. Visualize
craters on the end of the wand.

Venus is very hot, so picture the sole of your shoe on fire. Venus has phases like the moon, so imagine the moon tied up in the laces of your shoe. There is sulfuric acid in Venus' atmosphere. Visualize acid eating through the tongue of your shoe.

By using this method, you crowd a lot of information into a few hooks. The factors you memorize obviously relate only to the planet whose hook you placed them on. It's a very effective system. Try it.

REMEMBERING WHAT TO DO

Have you ever had the situation where your boss stops you when you're on the way somewhere, and asks you to do something when you get back? Or maybe someone asks you to check into something when you get a chance. And you don't want to forget to stop and get the clothes at the cleaners, and you have to call and order tickets for the concert.

How do you remember these things if you don't have a way to write them down. One way is to have "To-Do Hooks." That is, have a short set of hooks just for remembering things you have to do. The hooks can be designed and personalized in any form you like. They can follow a theme such as time-pieces, sports, containers, etc. You only need one set.

These hooks are just there to hold the items until you can write them down on your calendar or To-Do list. I always recommend keeping a list of the things you need to accomplish. If you forget just one out of a hundred of these things, it still may be the most important one. Write them down.

Time, time, time:

Your To-Do hooks can be something related to time-keeping, such as:

sundial	
pocket watch	
wrist watch	
alarm clock	
grandfather clock	
calendar	

Now, if you have cleaning to pick up, you can picture the laundry draped over the sundial. Your boss asks you to check on the sales figures, so you picture your pocket watch sailing in a pond. Then you are asked to fax a copy of a particular document when you get back to the office. You picture feeding your watch into the fax machine. Oh, and you need to call and order concert tickets. Those tickets are pictured between the bells of the alarm clock and the clapper.

When you get back to your To-Do list, you see the sundial, it has laundry on it. You see the pocket watch and it is sailing, etc.

Memorable attire:

Another approach is to use your clothing. One possible arrangement is

shoes	
socks	
trousers	
shirt	
underwear	
hat	

Now when you have to pick up the cleaning you picture the items crammed into or caught on your shoes. When you are asked to get the sales figures, picture your socks as sails on a boat. Imagine your trousers coming through the fax machine to remind you to fax the document. Finally, picture the concert tickets buttoned onto your shirt.

Everything but the kitchen sink:

Some folks use a place they are familiar with to memorize things they need to do. If you like to cook you can use your kitchen. You might put the items on your stove, in your refrigerator, down the garbage disposal, or in the kitchen sink.

If you like to work in the yard, you could use the mower, the trimmer, the clippers etc.

If you work with wood, you could use your different power tools or clamps or a vice as places to imagine your to-dos.

Wearing several hats:

One fellow I know remarked once about how many hats he had to wear at his place of work. After a little discussion he started using different hats as hooks to put things he had to get done. He actually made a little game out of what hat he would put things in. The fun of the game made it easier to remember the items.

When asked to pick up groceries after work he would say, "I'll put on my butcher's hat." Then he would imagine himself driving home in a butcher's or grocer's cap and apron. He would actually see how difficult it would be to put the seat belt on with the cap and apron in place. When he got into the car to go home, the image would come back and he would remember to get the groceries.

If a problem came up at work that he needed to get to soon but not immediately, he would put it in his fireman's hat. If somebody asked him to do something that was nearly impossible, he would put it in a magician's top hat.

Silly requests would be put under a clown's pointed hat. Financial matters would be put under a green eyeshade.

The whimsical approach:

Some people use their favorite cartoons as auxiliary hooks. "Hagar the Horrible," "Snoopy," " Mickey Mouse," and "Calvin and Hobbes" hold information for them. The funny situations that these characters get into, help to bring the items back to mind.

For instance, if you read the comics in your newspaper on a regular basis, you probably know the order of them on the page. Assuming that the comic at the top left of the page is "Snoopy," you could picture the first thing you want to remember in his doghouse or on a cactus. If "Dick Tracy" is next, picture the next item on his two-way wrist radio. If "Dennis the Menace" is next, picture Dennis giving the item to Margaret or Mr. Wilson.

En-Garde:

People of a more militaristic bent can use weapons of various types to defeat the projects that menace them. A club, sword, pistol, machine gun, cannon, and nuclear bomb should handle most lists.

A sporting chance:

For the sports fan there are the accoutrements of their favorite sports. A football goal post, hockey puck, pitcher's mound, golf club, ski poles, running shoes, etc. would offer some examples.

Memorizing your calendar

If you would like to know how to memorize your appointments and meeting times, stop and think about it for a minute. This is one of those areas where a written or electronic means of recall is superior.

If you are delivering a presentation and you forget one or two facts out of a hundred, it's okay. In fact, you will still appear to have a very good command of the topic. If you miss one appointment out of a hundred, however, it can be catastrophic. You may stand to lose a customer, promotion, job or reputation.

If it happens twice in a month you will appear to be unreliable. People will become upset. No one can afford to have a 99% success ratio in making his or her appointments.

I do not recommend using your memory as your calendar. If you are at all busy you must keep a written record of your appointments. This is a shared memory. Other people have a stake in this information. When there is a dispute, they will trust anyone's written word to your memory.

Get a good quality planner or calendar and keep meticulous notes of your appointments. There are electronic organizers now, too. These are very good at keeping track of appointments, contacts, minutes, and files.

Whatever method you use, get into the habit of including with each entry, where it is, when it is, who will be there, and what you need to bring. This will save a lot of guesswork.

If you have preparation before a meeting, be sure to schedule in the time for preparation.

Each day, go over the engagements for that day and the next. Each Monday, go over the whole week's events. Memorize them if you wish, but always check your calendar.

Where did I put...:

Some people believe that there is a land somewhere that contains all of the lost articles that we cannot find. Some say there are gremlins who steal the articles and secret them away. I've even heard it said that at the end of the world, all lost articles will be returned. Most of us can't wait that long.

We all know that things seem to disappear only to be found later when we are not looking for them.

Where are my Glasses?

How many times have you asked, "Where are my glasses?" or "Where are my car keys?" or, "Where are the scissors?" We often forget where we put simple articles.

No matter how we strain our brain, we can't remember where we put the thing. Some people go through an inventory of places they normally put the item. They frequently look in every place on the list several times. Some folks say a prayer to a patron saint, or recite a poem that is supposed to bring us luck in finding things.

It's no mystery why we misplace things. We simply don't pay attention when we set them down. There is no association in our memory between the thing and its location.

Thinking about the thing doesn't help us to recall where it is.

In order to remember where we put things we need a strategy that forms an association between the thing and its location. Here are a few approaches.

WAYS TO REMEMBER

Overloading:

Some people take the approach of overloading their environment with the item they can't find. Buy several pairs of glasses and pepper them around in briefcases, purse, dresser drawers, desks, etc. This is a little easier if you just wear reading glasses from the pharmacy. If you need prescription glasses this solution is obviously too expensive.

If you seldom use a flashlight, it may be hard to find one when you need it. The fact that it is often dark when you need it compounds the problem. Some folks go out and buy a package of small, inexpensive flashlights and put one in every room. When a storm knocks the lights out, they are never far from a flashlight.

A place for everything, and everything in its place:

It is much easier to find items if you always put the items in the same place. Assign a place for your glasses or keys. If it is at home that you tend to lose them, give yourself five or six places where you can lay down your glasses. Then, don't allow yourself to lay them anywhere else.

Whatever it is that you lose frequently, assign a place for it. If it is scissors, have a place or places for scissors and forbid yourself to lay them any place else. Whenever you finish the project with the scissors, put them in their place. Soon you will start to feel where the scissors are. You will think of them as out of place when you see or leave them somewhere else. This will cut down on the time you spend hunting for scissors or glasses.

Association:

A good mnemonic approach to remembering where we put things is to make a silly image when you set them down. If you put your car keys on top of the refrigerator, picture them cold and icy. Then when you reach for your keys the image of cold will remind you of the refrigerator. If you put them down on the coffee table, picture them scratching the coffee table. This will bring their location back to mind when you need them.

Try to vary the images that you use so there is no confusion. The next time the keys go on the coffee table imagine that they sink into the tabletop, or visualize them unlocking the table, or floating above the table. The newest, freshest image will always be obvious. As you develop this habit, you will stop forgetting where things are.

Remembering to bring something:

In my early days as a magician I was performing with several other entertainers at the Orpheum theatre. Our act was on last, so we got the props and illusions set up backstage and went down to the dressing room to get dressed.

As I unzipped the garment bag containing my tuxedo, it was obvious that there was no white shirt there. I panicked. I knew I ironed the shirt, but it must still be hanging in the laundry room. One of the other entertainers offered to loan me his white shirt, but it was too small.

My dear wife jumped in the car and drove across town at breakneck speed. She found the shirt right where I had left it and raced back to the theatre. She surely broke several traffic laws and double-parked to boot. She arrived as the emcee took stage. I threw on the shirt as I was being introduced. I tucked it in, fastened the studs and cufflinks, and pulled on my vest and jacket just in time. I was able walk on stage as if nothing had happened, but I was dripping with sweat and barely able to keep from shaking.

I still hear jokes about that day, but I never again forgot my shirt. The whole embarrassing event did teach me a valuable memory trick. The lesson is this. ***We tend not to repeat our most embarrassing mistakes.***

We can use that principle to help us remember what to bring or what to prepare for an event. The trick is to fantasize the embarrassing moment instead of living it. It is called mental rehearsal.

I now make it a point to imagine the worst possible scenario. I ask myself what would happen if I forgot to bring or prepare something. The emotion of rehearsing that, reminds me in the future of what I need to do.

I have imagined what it would be like to show up without my shoes, or microphone, or certain props. For sales calls I've pictured myself showing up without business cards, brochures, brief case, day planner, etc. It works.

Checklist:

Of course the other side of this coin is that we need to have checklists for the things we need. We can use written checklists, mental checklists or default checklists.

Written checklist:

A checklist is part of the planning stage for most new projects. We write down what we will need for a particular event or undertaking. If we put this checklist into the container we're going to use to carry the items, we can easily check for missing items. For repeat activities you can print a little card with the checklist and have it laminated.

Mental checklist:

After my harrowing experience at the Orpheum, I mentally go through my wardrobe whenever I pack. I picture shoes, socks, trousers, etc. until I have accounted for every item I will need. It has saved me untold grief.

For other projects a checklist can be memorized on a set of hooks or in a simple saying. This is why the reporter asks all of the 'W' words first, who, what, where, when and why. The patrolman who radios back to headquarters about a vehicle might use the word 'CYMBOL' to remember color, year, make, body style, occupants, license number.

Let's say for a particular type of call we need the following items:

Planner
Brochures
References
Samples
Forms
Business cards
Pen
Demo

You could use eight hooks, for just that purpose. Merely picture the necessary item in association with the hook. Here's a new set of hooks to use.

#	HOOK	ITEM	IMAGE
1	ton	planner	Planner weighs a ton
2	new	brochures	Brochures are wrapped as a present.
3	me	references	Yourself carrying reference books
4	roar	samples	A roaring tiger guarding your samples
5	live	forms	Live electrical wire igniting your forms
6	chicks	business cards	Chicks handing out business cards
7	cave in	pen	A cave-in on your pen.
8	fate	demo	Demonstrating a crystal ball

Exercises

Hooks Exercise 1

Use the formal hooks to memorize the constellations of the zodiac.

HOOK	CONSTELLATION	POSSIBLE IMAGE
1. Conductor's Wand	Aries The Ram	
2. Tuxedo Shoe	Taurus The Bull	
3. Tree On An Estate	Gemini The Twins	
4. Marble Floor	Cancer The Crab	
5. Queen Bee	Leo The Lion	
6. Peacock Chicks	Virgo The Virgin	
7. Golden Stairs	Libra The Scales	
8. Courthouse Doors	Scorpio The Scorpion	
9. Champagne	Sagittarius The Archer	
10. Fountain Pen	Capricorn The Goat	
11. Unleavened Bread	Aquarius The Water Bearer	
12. Elegant Shelf	Pisces The Fishes	

***

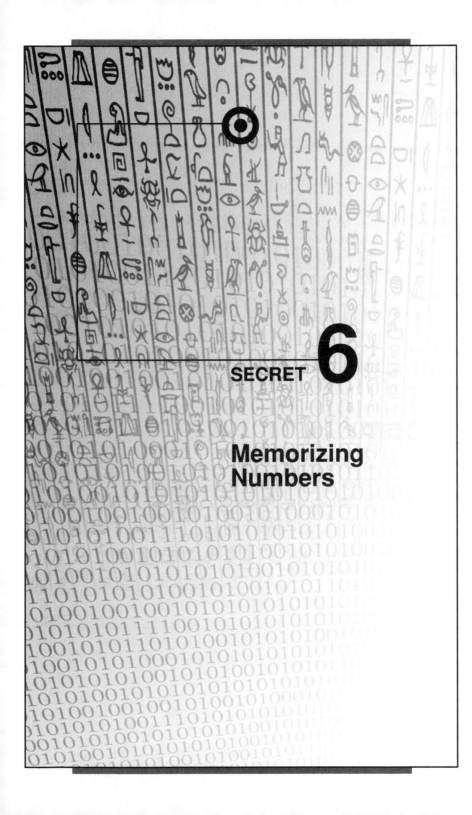

SECRET 6

Memorizing
Numbers

SECRET 6
Memorizing Numbers

A rt, a sales manager for a company that manufactures pumps, has a flawless memory for numbers. In his presentations he knows all the statistics by heart. He doesn't even look at the overheads, but quotes the flow ratios, churn rates, and price information precisely. Clients marvel at his product knowledge. He can easily quote the gallons per minute or friction loss of his competition as well as his own products. People don't argue about numbers with Art. They just expect him to be right.

Obviously, Art has a system.

Many people treat numbers as hieroglyphics. They are seen but not understood. No attempt is made to remember them. We simply write them down. Wouldn't it be wonderful if we could just remember numbers? We would know people's phone numbers. We would remember prices, part numbers, passwords, pin numbers, codes, ratios, formulae, and be able to work with numbers easily.

There is a way. In fact, there are several ways. We will look at two of the most popular ways to remember numbers. You can choose which one you like best. The first is the easiest to learn. The second one takes longer, but is much more flexible and allows you to do a lot more. I highly recommend using the second system if you will be dealing with a lot of information in the future.

Both of these systems are very old. There are records of a form of the second system as far back as the early books of the bible. This was before the Hebrew people had a written language.

A similar system was used in Persian literature during the 5th century BC. It is even more useful today than it was back then.

The reason that we have trouble remembering numbers is that they lack meaning to us. Numbers are just combinations of digits. Though most of us work with only ten digits, there are literally an infinite number of combinations of these digits. Although we know the system by which they combine we don't hold all of those combinations in our mind. That would be a terrible waste of space. So, any given combination does not mean much to us. If each number had an image, it would be much easier to remember.

DIGITAL WORDS

In eighteenth century England school children could "calculate" the first 20 digits of PI mentally. PI as you know is the relationship of the diameter of a circle to the circumference. The value that we use, 22/7, is wrong by the third decimal place. The actual value is 3.14159265358979323846.

Few of us could calculate that value today. Our calculators only have eight spaces.

Actually those English kids had a trick. They didn't really calculate PI, they remembered it. In fact, they memorized a poem that went like this:

Pie, I wish I could determine PI. Eureka, cried the great inventor, Christmas pudding, Christmas pie is the problem's very center.

Take a minute to see if you can figure out how it works. Why does that poem represent the number above?

If you got it, good for you. If you didn't or don't want to figure out the puzzle of it, here it is:

The number of letters in each word is the digit that it represents. "Pie" has 3 letters. "I" has 1 letter. "Wish" has 4 letters, etc., etc. Each word, therefore, very precisely represents its respective digit.

This method of remembering numbers is beautiful in its simplicity. We are already familiar with words; we can count the number of letters with a little practice. Certainly, poems and phrases are easier to remember than a string of numbers. Let's call this method "digital words".

According to this system, if we wanted to memorize a 4 digit number we would make a four word sentence or phrase that is made up of words that are the right length to represent the digits. Let's say that a PIN number is 4223. You could remember that by saying, "this is my pin." Each word has the proper number of letters in the proper order to represent the digits.

4	2	2	3
This	is	my	pin.

That, of course, was an easy example. Let's try a harder one. Bob's phone number is 467-4582. Remember that we not only need to memorize the number, we need to associate it with Bob. Therefore, we should try to get his name into the phrase. There are no three-letter words here so we could use "Bob's" for the four, or we could use 'Robert' for the six. Here arc a couple possibilities.

4	6	7	4	5	8	2
Bob's	number	belongs	here,	where	calendar	is.
4	6	7	4	5	8	2
Call	Robert	shortly.	Long	calls	frighten	me.

The sentence or phrase doesn't have to be a literary master-piece, or even be grammatically correct. It merely has to be easily remembered in its exact form.

Those of us who use automatic teller machines or telephone calling cards, need to remember the number codes. If we use computers on a network we need to update our pass-word every 30 days. We are told that, for security reasons, we should not use obvious things like our middle name, birthday, or social security numbers. Still, we need to be able to remember it. The banks and credit card companies let you set your own PIN number.

This system is great for coming up with passwords or pin num-bers that are unique and easy to recall. Just think up a sentence that you can remember and convert it to numbers. If you are environmentally inclined you could use "Save the whales." Or, you could use a sentence that has the name or something to do with the account. Something like these would do.

Third	National	Bank	Number
5	8	4	6
My	checks	don't	bounce.
2	6	4	6
Credit	Cards	Charge	Interest
6	5	6	8

For your medical insurance account you could use:

an	apple	every	day.
2	5	5	3

Your computer password could be:

Enter	password	and	hit	any	key
5	8	3	3	3	3

This way you can always remember your password or number.

Many people practice and develop this system as their main way of remembering numbers. They quickly become very aware of how many letters there are in every word. They also keep a horde of seven, eight and nine letter words. There are, of course, only a few one-letter words. 'I', 'O', and 'A' pretty well cover it.

A problem arises when you run into a number that has a zero in it. There are no zero letter words. There are two common ways of handling this dilemma. You could treat any word that means nothing as a zero. Therefore, "nothing," "none," "empty," "zip," and "zero" would mean zero. It becomes important now that you don't use these words for any other numbers.

101

The second method is to use the concept of zero degrees Fahrenheit. If the temperature is zero, it is cold. So any word that means cold could be used as zero. That could include, "chill," "frozen," "ice," and "snow."

You should only use one of these methods, not both. And the concept you decide on should be reserved only for zero letter words. For instance, if you use the cold method, "Bill has a cold forehead," could only be used to mean 43108, not 43148.

"Digital words" is a passable way to remember numbers if you don't have a lot to remember. However, if you want to be able to remember a lot of information of all kinds, I would highly recommend the next method. The Alpha-numeric system forms the basis for some very powerful memory systems, which we will see in the following chapters.

MEMORIZING NUMBERS ANOTHER WAY
THE ALPHA-NUMERIC SYSTEM

Thousands of years ago, methods were developed for dealing with complex information. Advanced systems of mathematics were refined long ago by cultures that didn't even have paper. Memory systems were also developed in antiquity. They were often interwoven with the mathematics of the time. One such system was used in ancient Middle Eastern cultures to mark the dates of their literature and scripture.

It is a form of that system that we will study next. The present system has been in use in England and the Americas for at least 150 years. The method is more economical than "Digital Words" in that it forms words to represent multi-digit numbers rather than sentences. It works by assigning sounds to the ten digits of our number system. We then put the sounds in the proper order to make words. This way the word "raincoat" can symbolize a number like 4271.

Here is how it works. The following sounds are first memorized. These sounds will be arranged in the proper order to form words, which are images for the numbers. The order of the sounds tell the order of the digits in the number which they represent

DIGIT	NUMBER
1	T or D
2	N
3	M
4	R
5	L
6	SH, CH, soft G, J, X
7	K or hard G
8	F or V
9	P or B
0	S or Z

Practice these sounds frequently. The system works best when the sounds have become second nature to the user. Be sure to practice all of the sounds for each digit. This will give you much more range. Where there is more than one sound for the digit, the sounds are really the same.

Families of sounds:

The sounds for one are formed in the same manner. Make the sound for 't' and then make the sound for 'd.' Notice that in each case the tip of the tongue goes against the front of the roof of the mouth and air passes across it.

The sounds for six are similar. The tongue forms a broad tube across the roof of the mouth and air is pushed through it for 'sh,' 'ch,' 'x,' soft 'g,' and 'j.' They are essentially the same sound.

For 'f' or 'v' the bottom lip is pulled up against the bottom of the top teeth and air is moved over it. Both sounds for eight are therefore the same.

Nine uses the 'p' and 'b' sounds. In both cases we put our two lips together and explode air through them.

The 's' and 'z' of zero are also formed in the same way. We form a tight tube of the tongue and the front of the mouth while we pull our lips open.

Understanding the concept of similar sounds for each letter makes it easier to remember them and to come up with appropriate words for the numbers.

Types of sounds:

All of the sounds in our system are consonants. There are no vowels. Only consonant sounds count in our system of numbers. There are three consonants that are not represented. They are 'w,' 'h' and 'y.' You might ask WHY? And that will help you remember which ones are not part of the system.

Putting the sounds to work:

The sounds for the numbers are arranged in words. It is important that they appear in the same order as the digits appear in the number. No other sounds from the list should occur in the word.

For instance, if we were to find a word to represent the number 'one' it would have either the 't' or 'd' sound and no other sounds from our list. It can have any number of vowels as long as it makes a word. The following words work well for 'one':

Day	Dye	Tee
Die	Hat	Tie
Doe	Hut	Toe
Dough	Tea	Wad

The reason that dough works even though it has a 'g' in it is because only the sound is important. The spelling is immaterial. These techniques were actually invented before there was a written alphabet. They remained popular in preliterate societies and with illiterate members of literate societies. Therefore, only the sound matters.

A silent letter does not count. Likewise, double letters count only once if you pronounce them as one sound.

The number 'two' could be represented by any word that has the 'n' sound and no others from the list. The following are examples:

Annie	Honey	Nay	Now
Hen	Knee	New	When
Hone	Know	Noah	Wine

Notice that each word has only the 'n' sound from our list and 'n' stands for 'two.' 'H' doesn't count and neither does 'W.' The "K" in knee and know is silent.

Now let's get a little more complex. The number 12 would consist of only the 't' or 'd' sound and the 'n' sound in that order. Some possibilities are:

Dane	Dune	Tiny	Tony
Dawn	Tan	Ton	Tune
Done	Tin	Tone	Wooden

Now if we reverse the order of digits and try to remember 21, we use the same sounds but in the opposite order. That would give us such words as:

Gnat	Knot	Node	Nude
Hand	Night	Not	Nut
Knit	Nod	Note	Wand

To represent the number we make a word or phrase that incorporates the sounds from our list in the order of the digits they represent. There are no other sounds from the list in the word or phrase.

Which of the words above for 21 do you think are best to remember the number? Which ones for 12?

If you chose nouns, you would be more likely to remember the numbers. To best recall items, we associate items.

Nouns usually form images mores readily than verbs or adjectives.

Try your hand on the following numbers. Put down a word for each number.

25	18	55	52
34	321	334	44
66	841	148	90

Now check your work. Are there any extra sounds? Did you use mother for 34 or cement for 321? Each of those has an extra sound from the list.

Here are some answers for the numbers. There are certainly many more.

25	nail	Nile	no lie	Nellie	knoll
34	mower	mare	mayor	hammer	merry
66	choo-choo	judge	jo jo	cha-cha	shoe show
18	dove	dive	taffy	toffee	daffy
321	mint	minute	mound	manta	mooned
841	fruit	fret	fort	ferret	varied
55	lily	lulu	lolly	whale oil	holy oil
334	mummer	my mower	my hammer	mommy hair	mime hare
148	turf	drive	tariff	trove	true half
52	lion	loin	lane	loony	loan
44	rower	roar	rear	hairy ear	error
90	buzz	bows	boys	base	bus

How did you do? If you missed a few, or even several, that's normal at this stage of the game. With just a little practice you will get much better. Each time you use an image for a number you add it to your mental vocabulary. After a while, words come to mind very easily for almost any number.

Some tricks to using the alpha-numeric system:

Number	Trick	Examples
Numbers starting with 1	The	144 = the rear, 11472 = the dragon
Numbers ending in 0	Plural	390 = mops, 9490 = burps
Numbers ending in 1	Past tense	811 = faded, 961 = bushed
Numbers ending in 27	Past participle	8527 = falling, 20127 = nesting
Numbers starting with 3	My	37410 = my carts, 3070 = my socks
Numbers starting 5	Low	5946 = low bridge, 59210 = low pants
Numbers ending in 4	-Er, one who does	614 = shooter, 94014 = burster
Numbers with double 0	Sauce, says	05002 = Sally says no, 3000 = moose sauce

From words to numbers:

Of course for the system to work, you must be able to convert words back into numbers. This is the easy part. When you have memorized, for instance, "Brief Passages" as Bob's phone number, you would picture Bob reading "Brief Passages." When you wanted to call Bob you would picture him and see "Brief Passages." This would tell you that his number was 948-9060.

"BRieF PaSSaGeS"

94 89 0 6 0

If your computer password was "73914" you would convert that to

CoMPuTeR

7 39 1 4

Try converting the following words to numbers:

Keystone	Speaker	Leopard
Car key	Nose ring	Fiddler
Basement	Shoestring	Jupiter
Blockhead	Potato chip	Dinosaur
Mouse tail	Ring	Newspaper
Kite string	Glasses	Donation

Here are the proper answers:

Keystone	7012	Speaker	.0974	Leopard	5941
Car key	747	Nose ring	20427	Fiddler	8154
Basement	90321	Shoestring	601427	Jupiter	6914
Blockhead	9571	Potato chip	91169	Dinosaur	1204
Mouse tail	3015	Ring	427	Newspaper	20994
Kite string	710-1427	Glasses	7500	Donation	1212

It will take time to become proficient with this system. Take a few minutes each day to practice converting numbers to words and words to numbers. You will be richly rewarded for that practice. Once you get it, it stays with you forever.

One good way to practice is to memorize all of your numbers and statistics.

- · License plate numbers. Yours, your family's, your friends
- · Social security number
- · Spouse's social security number
- · Kid's social security
- · Passwords
- · Pin numbers
- · Calling card number
- · Phone numbers
- · Prices when comparison shopping
- · Part numbers
- · Model numbers

Keep a list of the things you memorize on a small card or paper. Review it a few times a day until you have the numbers down pat. Bear in mind that the application of this system goes well beyond merely memorizing numbers. When you are practiced at this you will be ready to set up very powerful memory banks in your mind. So, practice changing numbers to words and words to numbers daily until it is second nature. You'll be glad you did.

Cheating on images:

The alpha-numeric system has been in existence for a very long time. You would think that by now someone would have written down images for the numbers. In fact, someone has. Actually many people have. Here then is a list of words that fit the system.

1. Tie		26. Notch		51. Lot		76. Cash
2. Noah		27. Neck		52. Lion		77. Cake
3. Ma		28. Knife		53. Loom		78. Coffee
4. Ray		29. Nap		54. Lure		79. Cap
5. Oil		30. Moose		55. Lily		80. Fuzz
6. Shoe		31. Mat		56. Leech		81. Foot
7. Cow		32. Moon		57. Log		82. Phone
8. Ivy		33. Mime		58. Lava		83. Foam
9. Bow		34. Mower		59. Lap		84. Fire
10. Toes		35. Mole		60. Chess		85. File
11. Toad		36. Mush		61. Sheet		86. Fish
12. Dawn		37. Mug		62. Chain		87. Fig
13. Tummy		38. Muff		63. Jam		88. Fife
14. Tar		39. Map		64. Cherry		89. Fob
15. Tile		40. Rice		65. Shell		90. Bus
16. Dish		41. Rat		66. Cha-Cha		91. Boat
17. Tack		42. Rain		67. Shack		92. Bun
18. Taffy		43. Rum		68. Chief		93. Bum
19. Tape		44. Rear		69. Chip		94. Bear
20. Nose		45. Rail		70. Gas		95. Ball
21. Knot		46. Rash		71. Coat		96. Beach
22. Nun		47. Rack		72. Coin		97. Book
23. Name		48. Roof		73. Cam		98. Buff
24. Wiener		49. Rope		74. Car		99. Pipe
25. Nail		50. Lace		75. Goal		100 Disease

When you are familiar with the alpha-numeric system, these words become very easy to remember. You then have ready images for two digit-numbers. By merely being familiar with these images, you can memorize small numbers very quickly.

111

They can also serve as a basis for constructing larger images for larger numbers.

Here is the special bonus. When you learn these 100 words that fit the system so well, you have a set of one hundred hooks!

MATHEMATICS

People say you can't memorize math, it must be understood. These folks seem to think that remembering and understanding are mutually exclusive concepts. In actuality a trained memory can serve you very well when studying mathematics.

In fact, before there were calculators, or even adding machines, mathematicians would memorize tables of numbers to reduce the amount of calculating they needed to do. The great Sir Edmond Haley (discoverer of Haley's comet) was known as a rapid calculator. He memorized tables of logarithms to give him greater speed in calculating orbital mechanics.

Many ancient and preliterate systems of mathematics rely on memorized information. Some very elegant systems allow people to do complex calculations in their head, or to use their body as an abacus. Farmers have tricks for quickly calculating the area of a piece of land and then the yield of that land and the price that yield will bring. Lumbermen have memorized tricks for computing board feet quickly in their heads. This is how a good memory aids you in the working of mathematics.

When you are first learning a given mathematical discipline all of the formulae can be daunting. It is, of course, vital that you understand each formula and what it accomplishes but you can only understand it if you remember it.

Until we understand a given formula, we need a way to hold it in our heads so we can work with it. When we remember it, it becomes part of our thinking and we understand it more clearly.

You can use any of several systems to memorize mathematical concepts. The Linking system will usually be the easiest to apply. Whichever system you use, however, will work much better if you first learn to use a system called "Sticky Words."

Sticky words:

Hooks are a way of making numbers into images. We can then use the hooks to memorize items in order. Similar to that concept is what we call "Sticky Words." Sticky words are images that we give to concepts that we are likely to use over and over again. They are just like hooks, but they symbolize the thing to be remembered, not the place we want to remember it.

Sticky words make the concept or item sticky like duct tape or Velcro. It does that by giving the concept an image. The image can be anything that will remind us of the concept. It could sound like, look like, or mean the same as the concept. For instance

The sticky word for Pi is Pie. A fresh apple pie is a whole lot easier to picture than the concept of Pi. A sticky word for minus is 'miners.'

A sticky word for $\sqrt{}$ is saxophone because of its shape. A sticky word for = is railroad tracks. The function of the sticky word is just to remind us of the concept. If we memorize the sticky words ahead of time it is easy to remember formulae. We merely assemble a link of sticky words or hang the sticky words on hooks.

Below is a table of common math operators and possible images to use as sticky words. Remember that the best sticky words are the ones that come back to mind easily. If something else comes to mind for a particular operator, by all means use it.

When you use the linking method to memorize a formula, it is good to have more than one sticky word for the common operators. You often need to use the same operator more than once in a formula. The table below has two "sound like' images and one 'looks like' image for each item. As you think up more, add them to your list.

STICKY WORDS FOR MATHEMATICAL OPERATORS [Use only one of the columns to memorize this formula.]			
Operator	Image (sounds like)	Image 2	Image 3 (looks like)
+	plows	Plug	Cross
−	miners	Midas	Line
±	Plaster Midas	Plaster mines	Cross on a board
/	slasher	Great divide	Fishing rod
*	Times (watches)	Time magazine	Star
=	eagles	Sequel	Railroad tracks
<	Lessor (Landlord)	Legs	Megaphone
>	Cheese grater	Road grader	Arrowhead
≥	At least (Leased)	More (moor)	Skater
≤	Up to (fill line)	No more	Duck call
≈	Around (a round of drinks)	About (a bout)	Waves
≠	Not (knot)	Nautical mile	Telephone pole
(	Left parent	Open parent	Satellite dish
)	Right parent	Closed parent	Lens
^	Power (muscles)	Power (Power boat)	Peak
√	Radical (Hippie)	Skateboard	Saxophone
x	some	Sumo wrestler	Clamp
π	pie	Pie pan	Table

Usually, the values that you are manipulating are represented by letters. You might encounter something like: 2X2+3Y=H. Fortunately there are sticky words for the letters as well. A list of them follows this section.

An algebra course will have lots of equations, which use a, b, c, or x, y and z. We can go further in this case and add hooks for the squares and cubes of these letters if needed.

115

The following is a list of possible sticky words for letter values and their powers. I would recommend that you only memorize the ones that come up in study. Don't memorize the whole list unnecessarily.

Letter	Image for Letter	Image for Square	Image for Cube
A	Ape	Apple	A-frame
B	Bee	Square bee	Beam of light
C	Sea	Seal	Seat
D	Deer	D-ring	Deep
E	Eel	Ear	East
F	Elf	Flag	Effervescence
G	Jeep	G-string	Gravity
H	Goal post	Hollywood	Halleluia
I	Eye	Square eye	I-beam
J	Jay	Jade	Javelin
K	Case	Kilogram	Kayak
L	Hell	L-train	Elbow
M	M&M	Ember	Empire
N	The end	Endive	Enemy
O	Doughnut	Inner tube	Life preserver
P	Peel	Pier	Peep show
Q	Cue card	Q-tip	Queue
R	Oar	Hour glass	Iron ore
S	Snake	S-curve	Estuary
T	Golf tee	Tea	Tee-shirt
U	Ewe	Yew tree	U-joint
V	Veal	Venus	Victory
W	Bubble gum	Double dip	Double standard
X	Ax	Railroad crossing	Ex-spouse
Y	Wire	Wine	Wild man
Z	Zebra	Zorro	Zenith

Now when you are faced with a formula, which is made up of these items, you can merely string them together with the linking system. Like cars on a train, each one will lead you to the next. Let's take a few examples.

Supposing you wanted to remember the formula for solving a quadratic equation.

$$x = \frac{-b \pm \sqrt{b^2 - 4ac}}{2a}$$

ITEM	STICKY WORD	LINK
quadratic	QUADS	Quad speakers.
x	AX	Ax chops the speakers.
=	EAGLES	Eagles carry off the ax.
-	MINERS	Miners shine their lights on the eagles.
b	BEE	Bee stings the miners under their helmets.
`	PLASTER MIDAS	King Midas turns bee into plaster.
Radical	HIPPIE	Midas turns hippie into plaster.
b2	SQUARE BEE	Square bee lands on hippie.
-	MINERS	Miners excavate square bee.
4	FLOOR	Miners are digging in the floor.
ac	OUTLET	There are electrical outlets in the floor.
Over	OVERALLS	Overalls are stuffed in the outlet.
2	DEW	Dew forms on the overalls.
a	APE	An ape is covered with dew.

Exercises

Numbers Exercise 1

Using the numbered hooks, memorize the remaining presidents in order. Form an image to remind you of each name and link it to the hook for the proper number. You can write your images in the columns below.

HOOK	PRESIDENT	IMAGE
11. Toad	Polk	
12. Dawn	Taylor	
13. Tummy	Fillmore	
14. Tar	Pierce	
15. Tile	Buchanan	
16. Dish	Lincoln	
17. Tack	Johnson	
18. Taffy	Grant	
19. Tape	Hayes	
20. Nose	Garfield	
21. Knot	Arthur	
22. Nun	Cleveland	
23. Name	Harrison	
24. Wiener	Cleveland	
25. Nail	McKinley	
26. Notch	Roosevelt	
27. Neck	Taft	
28. Knife	Wilson	
29. Nap	Harding	
30. Moose	Coolidge	
31. Mat	Hoover	
32. Moon	Roosevelt	
33. Mime	Truman	
34. Mower	Eisenhower	
35. Mole	Kennedy	
36. Mush	Johnson	
37. Mug	Nixon	
38. Muff	Ford	
39. Map	Carter	
40. Rice	Reagan	
41. Rat	Bush	
42. Rain	Clinton	

Numbers Exercise 2

Memorize the following dates of inventions using the number system you prefer.

ITEM	YEAR	IMAGE FOR YEAR
Toilet paper	589	
Pocket watch	1502	
Telescope	1608	
Submarine	1620	
Adding machine	1642	
Steam locomotive	1814	
Sewing machine	1846	
Color photography	1907	
Typewriter	1914	

Numbers Exercise 3

Memorize the squares for the first 20 numbers.

#	IMAGE FOR #	SQUARE	IMAGE FOR SQUARE
1		1	
2		4	
3		9	
4		16	
5		25	
6		36	
7		49	
8		64	
9		81	
10		100	
11		121	
12		144	
13		169	
14		196	
15		225	
16		256	
17		289	
18		324	
19		361	
20		400	

***

SECRET 7

Memorizing Names

SECRET 7
Memorizing Names

It is hard to overestimate the benefit of remembering people's names. We all feel a different affinity to people who call us by name. Those who usually speak our name are people that we know. They are our families, friends, colleagues, and acquaintances. So, when you remember someone's name shortly after meeting him or her, you make it easier to build a relationship with them.

To each of us the sound of our own name is the most recognizable words we will ever hear. We are conditioned from infancy to respond to our own name. We subconsciously associate it with the smiling faces of loved ones. Experiments have shown that people in noisy environments can hear their own name at a sound level lower than the ambient noise.

Every good salesperson is keenly aware of this. The use of a client or prospect's name is absolutely crucial to building a good working relationship. Teachers will tell you that they begin to get better cooperation from the class as they get to know each child's name.

So remembering names is one tool that helps to quickly build and maintain relationships.

OVERCOMING OBSTACLES:

Names though, are one of the more difficult challenges to the memory. We face many obstacles to remembering a name before we even attempt to memorize it. Let's look at what those obstacles are and how we can overcome them.

Obstacle one: Hearing the name

Perhaps the biggest obstacle to remembering names is the one that occurs at the moment of introduction. Believe it or not, we often fail to remember a name because we do not hear it. The name having never penetrated our brain leaves no impression.

Frequently, we literally do not hear the name. Have you ever introduced yourself to someone, "Hi, I'm Bob Jones." They reply by saying, "Hi, what company are you with?" or, "Are you the Bob Jones from Kansas City?" The reply does not include their name? You may chat for several minutes and then part without ever hearing the name. Later you will wonder why you don't remember their name. You never heard it.

Obstacle two: Getting the name

Sometimes we are introduced to someone and they either speak very softly or they mumble their name as they shake your hand. Perhaps they are nibbling on an hors d'oeuvre or are stifling a cough. The result is that you don't hear the name. In each of these instances you must stop and ask the person to repeat their name. Otherwise, you will never remember it. You may have to ask them more than once.

Some people are quite shy and downplay their name. They almost whisper it, if they give it at all. With these people you will have to make an effort to get the name. They will be amazed when you remember their names. Very few people ever do.

Obstacle Three: Holding the name

From time to time at parties, we are introduced to 5 or 6 people in a row. By the time you hear the fourth name, you have lost the first three. This is to be expected. Do not be afraid to go back and ask them individually for their names. You must hear and register the name if you are to remember it.

Normally when we are introduced, people do tell us their name with crystal clarity. However, as the sound of that name passes our ears, we are actually thinking of something else. Our mind is otherwise occupied. We may be trying to come up with some witty thing to say to this person. Or, we may be trying to guess what this person thinks of us or why he or she wants to meet us. Because we are not really paying attention, the name goes right by us.

We all do this. It is a hard habit to break. Overcoming this one obstacle, though, will greatly increase the number of names you remember. Force yourself, when you meet people, to concentrate on their names. At the moment of introduction, put everything else out of your mind. Listen to the name. Think of it as you hear it.

It is very helpful to make a habit of repeating the name. Call the person by name. You might even engage them in conversation

125

about the name. Find out how it is spelled. What is its derivation or ancestry? The more you deal with the name the better you will remember it. Call them by name when you part. All of these steps force you to pay attention to the name as you are talking to the person. This increases the associations between that person and his or her name.

So, the first and most important step in remembering a name is to overcome those four obstacles. If a person doesn't tell you his or her name, you must ask for it. If they mumble the name or it is difficult to pronounce you must have them repeat it. If you meet several people in a row, go back and ask their names. You will not remember a name that you never really hear. Pay attention to the name and use it in conversation.

Memorizing the name

Now we have overcome the great obstacles to remembering names.

The next step is to memorize the name. Remember our basic principle of mnemonics: **"Whenever two items are pictured in a silly, painful, or embarrassing association the thought of one automatically recalls the other."** In this case, the two things you have to deal with are the name and the face. Let's see how we can get a picture for each and then link them together.

THE NAME:

We don't think of names as images, though some actually are. If you met a Mr. Chuck Waggin for instance, his name would not be hard to picture. Neither would Ms. Sandy Banks or Mr. Phil Potts. Most names, however, are not pictures.

Our American culture takes names from all over the world. Among your acquaintances there are probably names from Poland, England, Ireland, Japan, Spain, America, Italy, China, Native America and countless other cultures. Those names often had real meaning in their original culture, but lost it in our polyglot of names. Some cultures name their children for specific animals or objects. Many last names actually refer to an occupation or a place. Someone named Cooper is probably descended from barrel makers. Mr. Miller comes from a family that used to grind grain. Some northern European cultures include forms of son or daughter as suffixes to denote relationships or lineage. Johnson, for instance, is actually "Son of John." O'Brien is "Of the Brien Clan."

Those relationships are not apparent to us in the profusion of names we find in America. We need to find another way to make names meaningful. That could be any image that somehow reminds us of the name. Thus, the name Smith might be pictured as a blacksmith. Watts could be a light bulb. Mary might be a little lamb.

Some names are easily associated with products. Wilson, for instance, could be tennis balls. Johnson could be baby powder. Clark could be candy bars or thread. In either case you have an image.

For those names that don't form an easy image it will be necessary to make one up that sounds like the name:

For a name like Gadzikowski, for example, you could picture a "gadget cow skiing."

For Newberg you could picture a "new burger." Knolls could be pictured as rolling hills.

A list of common names with suggested images follow this chapter.

THE FACE

Remembering a person's face is seldom difficult. It's right in front of us when we meet. Everyone will have the same face the next time we meet. We generally remember faces very well. In fact, a portion of our brain is dedicated to remembering faces.

However, a face is a very complex picture with lots of parts. We don't need to put the whole thing in our memories.

Each face has one component that catches our attention more than the other parts.

It may be the eyes, or the cheekbones, or even a scar. That's the part to focus on. As you look at a face you must decide, "what is the most outstanding feature of that face?"

Consider the lovely lady to our left. She has a very pleasing face and we would remember it. We might not, however, remember her name.

The face itself is an awful lot of information. Without realizing it we take in the whole face. We see the hair, eyes, chin, nose, cheeks, jaw line, etc. without separating them. At the same time we are unconsciously reading and evaluating the body language of the face and the body as well.

Our formula for memorizing calls for us to associate two images in a picture. The face is just too complicated to be one of those images

Just one component of the face would be much easier to picture. Look at the components of the same face on the next page.

Each component is distinctive, but one of them probably catches your attention more easily than the others.

129

Look for instance at the forehead. It has a recognizable shape and texture to it.

Maybe it's the size and shape of the eyebrows that grab your attention.

The eyes are the most expressive part of the face. Perhaps their shape and tilt attract your gaze. Or, perhaps they have a distinctive color.

Ann has high rounded cheekbones. That might be the part that you see first.

The nose can be very distinctive. Noses vary considerably in shape and size.

Ann's lips are pretty. They are thin, straight and composed.

It might be the lips which are the most outstanding component to you.

The trick is to pick just one component and use it to attach your image of the name. Let's assume you choose the lips as the part of the face that most grabs your attention. Picture the image for her name on that prominent part of the face.

This lady's name is Ann. A good image for Ann might be "ant."

Putting the name and face together

Once the name and the face have been assigned images they must be associated. To do that just picture the image for the name on the most prominent feature of the person's face. If Mr. Gadzikowski has a long thin nose you might picture the 'Gadget Cow skiing' right down that nose. If Ms. Newberg has dimpled cheeks you could picture a new hamburger stuffed in one of the dimples.

Of course, you will need to repeat the associations you make in order for them to stick in your mind.

The whole process will be hard at first, but will get easier as you do it. Eventually, you will already have images for most names you encounter. Practice makes perfect, so try your hand at the eight pictures on the next two pages.

1. Pick out the most prominent portion of the face, the part that grabs your attention.
2. Make an image for the name. Consult the list if you have problems coming up with an image for a given name.
3. Link the image for the name with the most prominent feature of the face.

Crystall Williams

Joe Pittman

Mark Darby

Scharlie Fitts

Mary Kay Mueller

Sylvia Kessler

Vern Wirka

Mark Peterson

Now recall the names of the same people. Look at the photos on the next two pages.

- Find the most prominent part of the face.
- Visualize the image that you pictured there.
- Recall the name.

If you missed a couple don't be discouraged. Go back and try again.

SAMPLE IMAGES FOR NAMES:

Last names

The following is a list of last names accompanied by images that will help in remembering them.

NAME	IMAGE	NAME	IMAGE
Achin	Aching	Braley	Braille
Adams	Apple	Branch	Branch
Anderson	Andirons	Brouillard	Brew lard
Arora	Aurora	Brown	Shoes
Bahr	Bar	Bruneau	Brown nose
Bailey	Bale, bridge	Buckles	Buckles
Baker	Baker	Burke	Burp
Bakhit	Batik	Byrd	Bird
Balak	Ball lock	Cabrera	Cab rear
Barbe	Doll, barb wire	Carlson	Curls on
Barber	Barber	Carper	Fisher for carp
Barnes	Barns	Cartensen	Cart in sun
Barrett	Barrette	Casarez	Case of rays
Barrier	Barrier	Casas	Houses
Bateman	Bait man	Cattano	Cat on 'o', sword
Beckner	Beak near	Celesky	Sell a ski
Beig	Big, beak	Cervantes	Serve ants
Bell	Bell	Christianson	Son of a christian
Bennett	Bend it	Conboy	Young con artist
Bisaillon	Bee sailing	Consier	Connoisseur
Blair	Loud speaker	Conway	Weighing a convict
Bloom	Bloom	Cook	Cook
Bodnar	Body near	Copenhaver	Cup in half
Boettger	Bet chair	Cravens	Cravings
Bowman	Bow man	Cross	Cross
Bradford	Bad ford	Darby	Derby

137

NAME	IMAGE	NAME	IMAGE
Davis	Goliath	Frescas	Fresca's
DeLancey	Take away lance	Frieze	Freeze
DeMaria	Divorce (de-marry)	Friis	Freeze
Dentler	Dent lair	Furrow	Furrow
DeTienne	Dead yen, detain	Gambhir	Gambler
Dickey	False collar	Gantt	Gander
Dieter	Deeder, dieter	Gerdes	Girdles
Diggins	Diggings	Godsey	God see
Dolezal	Doe will saw	Goodwin	Good wind
Dorman	Door man	Gordon	Flash, gourd
Dorn	Dorm, darn socks	Gray	Grey hair
Dostal	Doe's tail	Green	Golf green
Dowler	Dowel maker	Grybko	Grip cold
Dozier	Dozer	Gwinn	Going
Duryea	Do ray	Haftings	Half things
Dyer	One who dies cloth	Hahn	Hand
Earl	Oil	Hall	Hall
Eglsaer	Egg sailor	Haney	Hay knee
Ellis	Island	Hankenson	Hanky and son
Ersen	Ears on	Hansen	Hand send
Eshelman	Egg shell man	Harper	Harpist
Evans	Heavens	Harrell	Hair oil
Exline	x-x-x-x-x-x-x	Harris	Hairs
Fainter	One who faints	Hartley	Heart lee
Farkas	Far away gas	Haskett	Ask it
Farrell	Fair oil	Haskin	Has kin
Fender	Fender	Hays	Haze
Fine	Fine	Hazen	Hazing
Fiscus	Viscous, fisticuffs	Helms	Helms
Fitts	Fist, fittings	Hemming	Sewing Hems
Fitzke	Fits Key	Heye	Hay, hi
Flott	Float	Hickling	Heckling

NAME	IMAGE	NAME	IMAGE
Hill	Hill	King	King
Hirtes	Hurts	Kisicki	Kiss icky
Hoeneman	Honey man	Knott	Knot
Hoeppner	Hop near	Konforst	Convict forest
Horner	Horn player	Konwinski	Convict wins ski
Hough	Huff	Koop	Chicken coop
Howard	Howitzer	Kudera	Chaldera
Hradsky	Radical ski	Latimer	Lot of mare
Hubbert	You burnt	Lauritson	Lower his son
Hunt	Hunt	Lawson	Son of law
Hunter	Hunt	Lehr	Lair
Hurd	Herd	LeManton	Lemon ton
Incontro	In coin throw	Lett	Lead
Inzauro	In zorro	Lewis	Loose
Ishii	Itchy	Lichtas	Licked us
Jackson	Small jack	Lind	Lint
Janda	Chantere	Lines	Lines
Jelinek	Jelly neck	Longsdorf	Long door off
Johnson	Baby powder	Lozier	Low seer
Jolliffe	Show lift	Lynch	Lynching
Jones	Bones, Davy Jones	Mackeprang	Make prank
Jurek	Jerk	Maddock	Mad dog
Kalin	Kale in	Magness	Magnets
Kallhoff	Call off	Mangianelli	Man gem alley
Kalskett	Cow's kit	Marshall	Marshal
Kantor	Canter	Martinez	Martin (bird)
Karnes	Corns	Mason	Jar
Keeler	Keel maker	Maynor	Main oar
Kelly	Green cloth	McAlpine	Nick alp
Kessler	Kiss Lure	McCann	Nicked can
Ketelsen	Kettle son	McGovern	Mitt covering
Killion	Killing	McKeen	Mickey in

139

NAME	IMAGE	NAME	IMAGE
McManus	Nicked man	Pitt	Pit
Merrill	Merry go round	Pittman	Man in pit
Midkiff	Mid skiff	Pomeroy	Pomeranian
Miles	Miles	Porter	Porter
Miller	Beer, moth	Powless	Wiithout pow
Miloni	Baloney	Pritchard	Preacher
Mindrup	Men drop	Ramsey	Ram sea
Monestero	Man is thrown	Ramsey	Ram sea
Moore	Moor, more	Reed	Reed
Moran	More hand	Reeves	Reefs
Morrison	More sun	Rhone	Rowing
Morrow	Marrow	Richt	Richter scale
Mueller	Mule Hair	Rischling	Rich link
Murray	Merry go round	Robins	Robins
Nath	Naphtha	Robinson	Son of a robin
Nelsen	Wrestling hold	Rodriguez	Rod rackets
Nichols	Nickels	Rogers	Roger rabbit
Nielsen	Kneels on	Rosario	Area of roses
Nocita	No cedar	Rosenbaum	Rose in balm
Nohava	No have A	Runyan	Run young
Novak	New vacuum	Rybin	Ripen
Novotny	New vat knee	Salazar	Salad czar
Ogren	Ogre grin	Sansbury	Without berries
Osby	Oz bee	Saxon	Sacks on
Owens	Awnings	Scholz	Shoals
Papst	Beer	Seefeld	Sea felt
Parks	Parks	Seffron	Saffron
Pearson	Piercing	Sells	Cells
Peterson	Pen bursting	Sharp	Knife
Petak	Pea tack	Shepherd	Shepherd
Pettis	Pets	Silkett	Silk
Pirruccello	Pure cello	Silvestrini	Silver string

NAME	IMAGE	NAME	IMAGE
Sinnett	Sin it	Volcek	Volt check
Sitti	Settee	Vollmer	Vole mare
Smith	Black smith	Walker	Walker
Smithhart	Metal heart	Walpus	Walrus
Sprouse	Sprouts	Ward	Hospital ward
Stenberg	Stained burger	Warren	Rabbit warren
Stillian	Still yen	Watson	Small light bulb
Stohlmann	Stolen man	Watt	Light bulb
Stone	Stone	Weeks	Calendar
Strum	Guitaur	Wells	Wells
Sulhoff	Sell off	Wheat	Wheat
Suski	Sue ski	White	White board, white knight
Svenningsen	Swinging son	Wirka	Worker
Swanda	Swan dive	Wiens	Wieners
Tangeman	Tangled man	Wilburn	Will burning
Tarsikes	Tar sacks	Wilson	Basketball
Thomas	Tom tom	Winheim	Win dime
Tiffany	Lamp, jewelry	Witt	Brains
Tory	Tory	Wolfe	Wolf
Trimble	Tremble, thimble	Woolridge	Rich sheep
Troxell	Truck sale	Wynn	Wind
Ulmer	Ulna	Yost	Host
VanHorn	Horn of a van	Young	Baby
Viacrucis	'V' shaped cruisers	Zeluf	'Z' shaped loaf

First names

First names can be just as difficult for some people to remember. Here is a list of potential images for the first names of women:

NAME	IMAGE	NAME	IMAGE
Aileen	Leaning 'A'	Danita	Dinner tie
Aletha	Lethal 'A'	Dawn	Dawn
Alisa	A lease	Deann	Education dean
Angela	Angel	Debby	Debutante
Angelica	Angel licker	Deborah	The borer
Ann	Ant	Delores	Sorrows
Barbara	Barb wire	Denise	Tennis
Bernadette	Burn a debt	Diana	Dying ant
Betty	Bet	Diane	Dying ant
Brandy	Brandy	Donetta	Donut
Brenda	Branded	Donna	Ton of
Carla	Curler	Donnette	Dinette
Carol	Xmas carols	Elizabeth	Tin lizzy
Carrie	Carry	Ella	Elevator
Cathy	Cat	Elsa	Eels
Ceclia	See seal	Erlinda	Hair lint
Celine	Ceiling	Ernestine	Earnest teen
Charity	Charity	Esther	Chemical
Charlene	Charred lean-to	Frances	France
Cheryl	Shore oil	Gabriella	Angel Gabriel
Christina	Baptism	Gail	Gale
Christine	Crisp teen	Genevieve	Generate
Christy	Crispy	Geshila	Geisha
Connie	Conning tower	Ginger	Ginger
Constance	Convict's stance	Gisela	Giselle
Crystal	Crystal	Gloria	Morning glories
Cynthia	Cinders	Gwenda	Go in to

NAME	IMAGE	NAME	IMAGE
Heather	Heather	Martha	Moth
Helen	...of Troy	Mary	Little lamb
Ingrid	Ingrate	Mary Kay	Make-up
Iyuana	Iguana	Michelle	My shell
Jane	Chain	Maureen	More rain
Janet	Jar net	Mia	Me
Janice	Jam ice	Michelle	My shell
Jayme	Blue jay hymn	Nancy	Antsy
Jennifer	Spinning jenny	Natalie	Gnat
Jessel	Jostle	Nila	Nile river
Jessica	Rabbit	Norma	Normal
Joann	Show ant	Olivia	Olive
Jocelyn	Jostling	Pamela	Pummel her
Jodi	Other lover	Patty	Patty (hamburger)
Joy	Happiness	Penny	Penny
Julie	Jewel	Priscilla	Prissy
Karen	Karo syrup	Raquel	Racket
Kathy	Cat	Rebecca	Real beggar
Kelli	Green cloth	Rita	Meter maid
Kenya	Kenya	Robin	Robin
Kimberly	Paper products	Rory	Roar
Kristen	Baptize	Rose	Rose
Kristine	Crisp teen	Ruby	Ruby
Linda	Lint	Sabrina	Witch
Lisa	Lease	Sally	Sully
Lois	Superman's friend	Sandra	Sander
Loni	Long knee	Sarah	Sarong
Loretta	Low rider	Shannel	Channel
Luis	Loose	Shannon	River
Marilynn	Barreling	Sharon	Sharing
Marjorie	Marjoram	Sheila	Shield
Marlene	Marlin (fish)	Shelly	Shell

The Lost Art of Human Memory

NAME	IMAGE	NAME	IMAGE
Sherri	Sherry wine	Tonya	Torn yo-yo
Sheryl	Shore oil	Tracy	Trace
Stacey	Stays	Treasure	Treasure
Stephanie	Stiff knee	Trena	Soup tureen
Sue	Sew	Twila	Twilight
Sylvia	Silver	Valerie	Valor
Tabitha	Tab eater	Vella	Vellum
Tamaga	Tomato	Veronica	Fur on a cow
Tammy	Dam	Vicki	Vicks
Teresa	Terry cloth	Wendy	Windy
Terri	Terry cloth	Yvonne	Even
Tina	Teen		

Now for men's names:

NAME	IMAGE	NAME	IMAGE
Alexander	The great	Delbert	Dilbert
Andre	Mints	Dennis	Tennis
Andrew	Ant drew	Derek	Derrick
Anthony	Ant throne	Donald	Duck
Arne	Arm	Douglas	Fir
Arthur	Author	Duane	Twang
Branden	Branding	Elliot	Elevator
Brian	Brine	Eric	Viking
Bruce	Bruise	Gary	Carrier
Charlie	Charcoal	Gregory	Gray gory
Chris	Crispy	Hakim	Hack him
Christian	Preacher	Howard	Howitzer
Clint	Flint	Jack	Car jack
Craig	Crag	James	Gym
Daniel	Lions den	Jason	Argonauts
Darrell	Barrell	Jay	Blue jay
David	Sling shot	Jeffrey	Chafe

NAME	IMAGE	NAME	IMAGE
Joe	Coffee	Randy	Brandy
Joel	Shoal	Raymond	Ray of light
John	Restroom	Richard	Rich (money)
Kenneth	Can	Robert	Rubber
Kevin	Cave in	Rodney	Rod
Kiran	Gear in	Roger	Short wave radio
Kirk	Space captain	Ron	Run
Kyle	Keel	Scott	Kilt
Lance	Lance	Steve	Stevedore
Lathan	Lathe	Thomas	Tom tom
Lemuel	Lemming	Tim	Timothy (spice)
Louie	Lew	Todd	Toddy
Marcel	Mime	Tony	Home permanent
Mark	Marker	Troy	Tray
Marlin	Fish	Victor	Victory
Mathew	Mat	Vern	Fern
Michael	Archangel	Wade	Wade in water
Neil	Kneeler	William	Bill

FUN STUFF

SPELLING

In these days of spell checkers and computers we don't need to be able to spell each word correctly. Indeed, the spell checker has shown many of us that our spelling of certain words was just plain wrong. Because we always thought that our spelling of a word was correct, it is very hard to remember the proper spelling even though we've seen it on the computer.

Fortunately, there are a myriad of ways to remember how to spell any word that gives you trouble.

Rules:

There are various rules for spelling English words. For instance:

I before E except after C, or in words that sound like A as in neighbor or sleigh.	believe, receive, receipt, etc.
The -ful suffix means full of and it always has one L.	thankful, spoonful, sorrowful
Always keep the Y when adding –ing.	flying, partying, playing
E's will ease on out before you add suffix.	baked, coming, raising

It is helpful to learn the major rules. We are taught some of them in grammar school.

There are, however, exceptions. Learning these can be tedious. We could easily memorize a lot of arcane rules for words that we already spell correctly or never use.

A sensible approach is to take words that you frequently misspell and learn a mnemonic for spelling each of those words. In time you will become a better speller.

Suppose you had trouble spelling "Separate." Many people do. The most common misspelling of "Separate" is to change the first A into an E, Seperate.

Let's look at a few different ways to make mnemonics for "Separate."

Pronounce:

Pronounce the word the way it is spelled: *Sep ay rate* or *Seh Par ate*.

By saying it a few times this way you will remember to use an A instead of an E.

Visualize:

Picture the word with the offending letter or letters exaggerated.

Separate, SepArate, **Separate**, SepArate

Silly Image:

Picture yourself as you Separate a rat. That reminds you there is a rat in Sep**arat**e.

Or imagine that you separate an A-Frame house, to remember the A.

Mentally separate an A.

Silly phrase:

Make up a phrase that reminds you of the proper spelling. This uses a word or phrase that has the proper of letters in it.

Sep**arate** the **A-Rate**.

Se**par**ate those on **Par**.

Se**para**te is a separate **para**graph.

There is **a rat** in sep**arat**e.

Another approach is to make a memorable sentence, which contains the word. It also spells the word in the first letter of each word of the sentence. For instance:

S   E   P   A   R A   T   E

Separate every purple and red ascot that exists.

S   E   P   A   R AT   E

Separate eels push and roll a turtle egg.

Let's try another word. "Privilege. "

The common misspellings of Privilege are Privlege, and Priviledge.

Pronounce:

Priv I leg e

Visualize:

Privilege,   PrivIlege,   **PRIViLEGE**,   Privi**lege**, Privi**LEGE**,

Silly Image:

Priv   I   leg e

  E

Silly phrase:

It is **vile** that the rich have such Pri**vile**ge.

There is no <u>ledge</u> with privi**lege**.

First word spelling:

P   R   I V   I   L   E   G   E

Privilege really is virtually immoral. Large estates generate envy.

You need not try all of these on a given word. Just take any one that works to bring back the proper spelling.

Spelling Exercise 1

Make up mnemonics for these frequently misspelled words.

WORD	PROBLEM	MNEMONICS
Procedure	-ced not ceed	
Knowledge	-dge-	
Tailor	-or- not –er-	
Raccoon	-cc-	
Paid	-aid- not –ayed-	

PLAYING CARDS

My wife's dear Aunt Cres is 90 years old. She is a woman of exceptional mental prowess. Woe unto the hapless soul who thinks they can beat her in a card game. Her cupboards are full of bridge trophies, won at the highest level of competition. At any point in the game, Aunt Cres knows exactly which cards have been played. She also has a very good idea who has which card. There are many other weapons in her mental arsenal, but memorizing the cards is fundamental to good card play.

Card players, magicians and gamblers should know how to keep precise track of cards played. You can do the same thing with the following system. It draws on the work you have already done. You must first learn a new set of sticky words, one for each card. Then you will learn how to mentally mark them quickly. Here are the sticky words for the cards,

STICKY WORDS FOR CARDS

	CLUBS	HEARTS	SPADES	DIAMONDS
A.	Clay	Hays	Sage	Dates
2.	Clue	Who	Sue	Dew
3.	Cleat	He	Sea	D-ring
4.	Core	Horse	Sore	Door
5.	Chive	Hive	Sieve	Dive
6.	Clicks	Hitch	Six pack	Ditch
7.	Cave in	Heaven	Seven (dice)	Divan
8.	Crate	Hate	Sadist	Date
9.	Kind	Hind	Sign	Dine
10.	Can	Hen	Scent	Den
J.	Club	Heart	Spade	Diamond
Q.	Clean	Queen	Steam	Dream
K.	King	Hinge	Sing	Ding

The first sound in each hook word is the first sound of the suit. H for hearts, D for diamonds, etc.

The second sound rhymes with the card. For instance the five of hearts is 'Hive." The hook for the eight of diamonds is

"Date." Some of the hooks don't quite rhyme. There we use something that comes close enough for us to remember it.

The jacks are all the name of the suit. The jack of clubs is a club, etc. The queens and kings were somewhat forced so you will have to just commit them to memory. The queen of hearts is the queen. The king of clubs is a king. The others either rhyme with or sound like queen or king.

Playing for tricks

This method is used for games where tricks are taken. This would include, bridge, pitch, etc. In the heat of play there is not time to memorize the cards. All you really need to do is mark them as played. This is done by mentally mutilating the cards.

For instance, if the jack of diamonds is played, just picture a diamond smashed to bits. If the king of clubs is played picture the king smashed. Then, when you want to play a diamond or a club picturing the king will show you the mutilation. The king has already been played. If there were no mutilation, the king would still be out.

For successive hands, use different mutilations. Fire could be one hand, flood another. Change the mutilation image for each hand so that you don't become confused.

Showing off

A rather showy demonstration of memory skill is to have someone take five cards out of the shuffled deck. Then have someone call off the remaining cards, or you look at the remaining cards. As you do so mentally mutilate the cards. When finished run through the suits card by card and you'll see which cards are missing. Announce the missing cards to the person holding them and everyone will be astounded.

Memorizing the deck

Once you learn the sticky words for cards, you can also memorize a shuffled deck of cards. Merely associate each successive card with the hook for the next number. If the first card is the queen of hearts, associate the queen with a tie. If the second card is a four of spades picture Noah with a sore. Continue on until the whole deck is memorized.

Other uses

The process of mentally mutilating the sticky words can be used for other things as well. When you set up a mental checklist for something, you can check them off the list by merely burning them, smashing them or cutting them in your mind.

If you find that you don't use the sticky words for card playing, you can use them as another set of 52 hooks.

Answers to Exercises:

The following are suggested images for the chapter exercises.

Linking

Linking Exercise 1

THE THIRTEEN ORIGINAL STATES

STATE	IMAGE FOR STATE	CONNECTION
Delaware	Underwear	Uncle Sam in his underwear
Pennsylvania	Pencil	Underwear on a pencil
New Jersey	Jersey	Jersey defaced with pencil marks
Georgia	Peach	Peach smeared on new jersey
Connecticut	Connector	Electrical connector in peach
Massachusetts	Message	Message sent over connector
Maryland	Bride (Marry)	Message delivered to bride
South Carolina	Confederate soldier	Bride runs off with confederate
New Hampshire	New Ham	Confederate soldier eating ham
Virginia	Gin	Ham soaked in gin
New York	Big apple	Apple in gin bottle
North Carolina	North pole	Big apple at the north pole
Rhode Island	Road	Road leading to north pole

Linking Exercise 2

The Eleven Confederate States

STATE	IMAGE FOR STATE	CONNECTION
Alabama	Album	Confederate flag in album
Arkansas	Ark	Pop-up ark in album.
Florida	Floor	Ark sailing on the floor
Georgia	Gorge	Gorge in floor
Louisiana	Mardi Gras	Mardi Gras in gorge
Mississippi	River	Mardi Gras crossing the river
North Carolina	North pole	North Pole sticking out of frozen river
South Carolina	Southern belle	Southern belle dancing around north pole
Tennessee	Tent	Southern belle in small tent
Texas	Taxes	People paying taxes in tent
Virginia	Fur chin	Tax forms on a fur chin

The Lost Art of Human Memory

Linking Exercise 3

Ages Of The Earth

AGES OF THE EARTH	IMAGE FOR AGE	CONNECTION
Pre Cambrian	Pretty Camper	A pretty camper on the earth
Cambrian	Camper	A boy scout (camper), comes out of the pretty camper
Ordovician	Ore division	Boy scout divides chunks of ore.
Silurian	Cellar Inn	Loads of ore are dumped in Cellar Inn
Devonian	Devotion	Prayer service held in Cellar Inn.
Pennsylvanian	Pencil	Everyone in prayer service is holding a large pencil
Permian	Permanent (Hair)	Giving someone 'perm' with pencils to hold the hair
Triassic	Dry Acid	Dry acid poured on perm
Jurassic	Jury	Sprinkle dry acid on a jury
Cretaceous	Crate Edges	Jury sitting on the edges of crates
Tertiary	Dirty Sherry	Crates are full of dirty sherry
Quaternary	Quarter Near	Quarters in the bottles of sherry

Linking Exercise 4

The ranking of hands in Poker

HAND	IMAGE	CONNECTION
Straight Flush	Water flushing down a long straight pipe	Cards flushing down pipe
Four of a kind	Golfer (Fore)	Golfer hits ball down pipe
Full House	House	Golf ball hits house
Flush	Toilet	House is flushed down toilet
Straight	Strait (Body of water between two islands)	Toilet floating down the strait
Three of a kind	Tree	Large tree growing out of strait
Two pairs	Two pears	Only two pears on tree
Pair	Paring knife	Paring knife slices both pears
No Pair	This is obvious	

Vocabulary Exercise 1

The classifications of Taxonomy from General to specific

CLASSIFI-CATION	IMAGE	CONNECTION
Kingdom	King	King walking through field of tacks (Taxonomy)
Phylum	File	King filing his nails
Class	Classroom	Kids in class filing their desks
Order	Military command	Soldiers in formation march into classroom
Family	Spouse and children	Soldiers standing in formation, have kids playing in the ranks
Genus	Genius	One of the children is a genius (large brained)
Species	Speakers	The genius is broadcasting on large speakers
Variation	Variety	Variety of sizes and shapes of speakers

The Lost Art of Human Memory

Vocabulary Exercise 2

Motions of the earth

MOTION	IMAGE	MEANING	IMAGE
Rotation	Row of potatoes (Row 'taters)	The earth spinning on its axis each day	A huge spinning **potato** instead of the **earth**
Revolution	Revolutionary War	The movement of the earth around the sun each year	**Soldiers** marching **around the sun**
Precession	Pre-recess	The circular motion of the axis, every 26,000 years (like a spinning top.)	Kids **spinning tops** before **recess**
Nutation	Newt aging	The slight wobble of the axis within the precession (every 19 years)	An **old newt wobbling**
Solar drift	Drifter	The sun bobs up and down in the galaxy	**Drifter bobbing up** and **down** in the galaxy
Galactic rotation	A Ford galaxy spinning	The whole galaxy rotates around its common center	A Ford **Galaxy spinning** with the **sun** on one end

158

Landmarks Exercise 1

Families of Shorebirds

SHORE BIRDS		
ITEM	PLACE	IMAGE
Shore birds	Kitchen	Shorebirds in your kitchen
Plovers	Chair	Pullovers on chair
Oystercatchers	Floor	Catching oysters on floor
Stilts	Doorway	Stilt-walkers in doorway
Jacanas	Table	Jackhammers on table
Sandpipers	Sink	Pipes made out of sand in sink
Turnstones	Sink drain	Turning stones in the drain
Surfbirds	Sink faucet	Birds surfing on the faucet
Phalaropes	Edge of sink	Falling ropes over edge of sink
Gulls	Stove	Gulls on stove
Jaegers	Burner	Jaguars laying on burner
Gulls	Knob	Gull turning knob
Terns	Pan	Pan turning over.
Skimmers	Oven	Bottle of skim milk in the oven
Alcids	Refrigerator	Alice sitting in refrigerator

Hooks Exercise 1

Constellations of the Zodiac

Hook	Constellation	Possible Image
1. Conductor's Wand	Aries The Ram	Wand tapping a hairy ram
2. Tuxedo Shoe	Taurus The Bull	Bull wearing tuxedo shoes
3. Tree On An Estate	Gemini The Twins	Twins climbing the tree
4. Marble Floor	Cancer The Crab	Cancerous crab on the marble floor
5. Queen Bee	Leo The Lion	Lion eating a queen bee
6. Peacock Chicks	Virgo The Virgin	Virgin surrounded by peacocks
7. Golden Stairs	Libra The Scales	Scale on each of the golden stairs
8. Courthouse Doors	Scorpio The Scorpion	Giant scorpion coming out courthouse doors
9. Champagne	Sagittarius The Archer	Champagne bottle hanging from archer's arrow is making it sag
10. Fountain Pen	Capricorn The Goat	Goat writing with fountain pen
11. Unleavened Bread	Aquarius The Water Bearer	Water carried on wafer of unleavened bread
12. Elegant Shelf	Pisces The Fishes	Wet flopping fish on shelf

Numbers Exercise 1

Presidents

HOOK	PRESIDENT	IMAGE
11 Toad	Polk	Poker
12. Dawn	Taylor	Tailor
13. Tummy	Fillmore	Fill mower
14. Tar	Pierce	Pierced ears
15. Tile	Buchanan	Blue cannon
16. Dish	Lincoln	Linking rings
17. Tack	Johnson	Small john
18. Taffy	Grant	Granite
19. Tape	Hayes	Hay
20. Nose	Garfield	The cat
21. Knot	Arthur	Author
22. Nun	Cleveland	Cleaver
23. Name	Harrison	Hairy son
24. Wiener	Cleveland	Cleaver
25. Nail	McKinley	My kindling
26. Notch	Roosevelt	Rosy felt
27. Neck	Taft	Taffeta
28. Knife	Wilson	Tennis ball
29. Nap	Harding	Hardened
30. Moose	Coolidge	Cooler
31. Mat	Hoover	Vacuum cleaner
32. Moon	Roosevelt	Rosy felt
33. Mime	Truman	True man
34. Mower	Eisenhower	Ice on tower
35. Mole	Kennedy	Candy
36. Mush	Johnson	Small john
37. Mug	Nixon	Nickers
38. Muff	Ford	Ford
39. Map	Carter	Cart
40. Rice	Reagan	Ray gun
41. Rat	Bush	Bush
42. Rain	Clinton	Glint

Numbers Exercise 2

Year of inventions

ITEM	YEAR	IMAGE FOR YEAR
Toilet paper	589	Leave up the toilet paper.
Pocket watch	1502	Doll son has pocket watch.
Telescope	1608	Teach safe use of telescope.
Submarine	1620	The submarine is caught in tie chains
Adding machine	1642	Dodge rain to keep adding machine dry.
Steam locomotive	1814	Locomotive has a tough tire instead of a wheel
Sewing machine	1846	Sew through a tough roach.
Color photography	1907	See a camera in your top sock.
Typewriter	1914	Typed hair.

Numbers Exercise 3

Memorize the squares for the first 20 numbers.

#	IMAGE FOR #	SQUARE	IMAGE FOR SQUARE
1	Tie	1	Tie on doe
2	Noah	4	Noah with lots of hair
3	Ma	9	Ma hit with a pie
4	Ray	16	Ray in a ditch
5	Oil	25	Oil floating down the Nile
6	Shoe	36	Shoe full of mush
7	Cow	49	Cow twirling a rope
8	Ivy	64	Ivy covering a chair
9	Bow	81	Bow on your foot
10	Toes	100	Toes with a disease
11	Toad	121	Toad in a tent
12	Dawn	144	Dawn on a terrier
13	Tummy	169	Tummy touch-up
14	Tar	196	Tar on the beach
15	Tile	225	Tile broken by new nail
16	Dish	256	Dish with a new latch
17	Tack	289	Tack in a navy pie
18	Taffy	324	Taffy found by a miner
19	Tape	361	Tape machete
20	Nose	400	Nose stuffed with roses

FUN STUFF

Spelling Exercise 1

Make up mnemonics for these frequently misspelled words.

WORD	PROBLEM	MNEMONICS
Procedure	-ced not ceed	We will do this procedure on **Ed**, PROCeDURE
Knowledge	-dge-	To have knowledge you must **know** the **ledge**
Tailor	-or- not –er-	A tailor sewing an '**O**' shaped suit.
Raccoon	-cc-	Raccoons looking out to sea. They **see sea**.
Paid	-aid- not –ayed-	If I don't get **paid**, you will need first **aid**.

CONCLUSION

At this point you have been exposed to several tricks, methods and systems for making your memory much stronger. Hopefully, you have practiced your favorite methods. By the time you have committed a hundred hooks to memory you will be a very able learner. Your proficiency will grow more rapidly as you continue to use these methods.

You are now equipped to learn at a much higher level. I would encourage you to enjoy your new mental powers as they develop. Memorize people's names and call them by name when you see them next. Deliver your presentations without written notes. Absorb the knowledge of classes and seminars. Study for the professional designations in your business or industry.

Our pleasures as humans are centered in our brains. To learn is one of the purest of pleasures. To know something new is very satisfying, but to know it quickly and in exquisite detail is exhilarating. Take time to savor the delight.

Teach your children.

Spread the word.

***

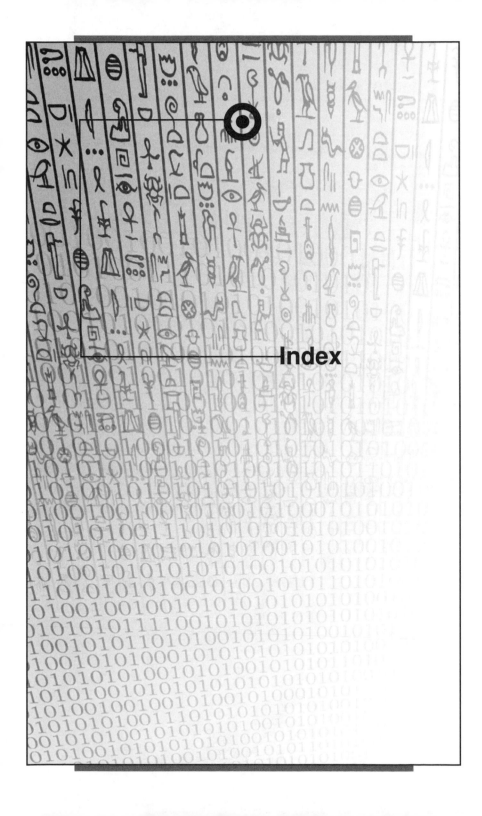

Index

The Lost Art of Human Memory

INDEX

Index

Now that you've discovered "The Lost Art of Human Memory," why not share it. This book makes a wonderful gift for your staff, your friends or anyone who loves to learn.

ORDER FORM

Please send

Book	Qty.	Price	Total
The Lost art of Human Memory		$14.95	$
Nebraska residents add 6.5% sales tax.			$
Shipping : 1 copy = $3.50 2 to 5 copies = $5.00 More than 5 copies = 6% of total cost			$
Total amount of order			$

Name _____

Company _____

Address _____

City _____ State _____ Zip _____

Phone (___) _____ Fax (___)_____

E-mail _____

Method of Payment:
☐ Check ☐ Money Order ☐ Visa ☐ MC

Account No. _____

Expires _____ Signature _____

Mail your order to: **TOPHAT PRESS**
P. O. Box 641888
Omaha NE 68164 USA

Or fax: **402 (571-0980)**
Or call: **1-877-841-2935**